$7.95

Marcus Reel

9-8-83

D1559552

Understanding the difficult words of Jesus

Understanding the difficult words of Jesus

David Bivin
Roy B. Blizzard

Published by
Makor Foundation
Arcadia, California 91006

Library of Congress Data 83-61850

Understanding the Difficult Words of Jesus
© 1983 Makor Foundation
Published by
Makor Foundation
Arcadia, California 91006

Illustrations by John J. Harrison
Printed in the United States of America

Cover Design by Dick Birkey
Isaiah Scroll Photograph
Compliments Dr. John Trever

To Our Parents

Mr. and Mrs. J.C. Bivin
Drumright, Oklahoma

Mr. and Mrs. Roy Blizzard, Sr.
Joplin, Missouri

Acknowledgments

We are indebted to many wonderful people whose keen interest in our research and whose love for the words of Jesus have made this book possible. Their number is legion and to mention each one would require a space much larger than that allotted. However, each one knows of their contribution and support, and to all we extend our grateful appreciation.

We must thank our wives, Josa Bivin and Gloria Blizzard, for their patience and encouragement. Only because they willingly shouldered an extra load of work over the past year was it possible for this book to be completed.

Lorne and Earline Blacklock deserve special mention for their encouragement and dedication to Israel research. Their conviction and devotion led to the founding of Makor Foundation, a non-profit foundation devoted to biblical research, of which Lorne is the president. We thank Makor Foundation for publishing this book, which we hope will be just the first in a series on

Understanding the Difficult Words of Jesus.

We wish to thank Dennis and Georgia Clifton for the many hours they devoted to editing and proofreading this manuscript, and Georgia Clifton for typing and re-typing the manuscript as well as preparing it in its final form for the publisher. Their contribution saved us many hours of labor.

We are especially indebted to Dr. Robert L. Lindsey and Professor David Flusser, whose collaboration has opened a new era in the field of New Testament re-search, and made Jerusalem a center for Synoptic* studies. Most of what we have learned about the sayings of Jesus is a result of their ground-breaking work.

We are also indebted to Halvor Ronning and Brad Young, both doctoral candidates under Professor Flusser's direction at the Hebrew University of Jerusalem. As members of what might today be called "the Jerusalem school of Synoptic research," they are constantly contributing to a better understanding of the text of the Gospels. Their countless discussions over the years with David Bivin have in no small way helped to shape this book.

We would like to express our gratitude to Randall Buth of Mbili, Sudan, who read the manuscript and made many valuable suggestions.

We are deeply grateful to the Israel Museum and the Israel Department of Antiquities for allowing us to re-produce photographs of archaeological artifacts in their possession. Special thanks is due to Irene Lewitt and Genya Markon of the Israel Museum's Department of

*Matthew, Mark, and Luke are known to scholars as the "Synoptic" Gospels.

Photo Services for their assistance in selecting photographs which would best illustrate the contents of the book. Our appreciation also goes to Dr. Magen Broshi, Curator of the D. Samuel and Jeane H. Gottesman Center for Biblical Manuscripts (The Shrine of the Book), for providing from his archives photographs of Dead Sea Scrolls and one of the Bar-Cochba letters, and to Dr. Ya'akov Meshorer, Curator of the Numismatic Department of the Israel Museum, for suggesting which of the Jewish coins to use as illustrations.

Contents

Bibliography

Foreward

It gives me pleasure to commend this book to those who desire a closer acquaintance with what Jesus said and did in Galilee and Judea at the beginning of the Christian era. Scholars David Bivin and Roy Blizzard have here provided an introduction to the basic question of how best to approach and understand the words of Jesus — whether by limiting ourselves to the translation of the Greek texts, preserved so faithfully by the Church, or by exploring more deeply into the Hebrew texts lying behind our Greek ones.

My own encounter with the strong Hebraism of the Gospels of Matthew, Mark, and Luke came several years ago when I had occasion to attempt the translation of the Gospel of Mark to Hebrew. What first caught my attention was the very Hebraic word order of the Greek text of Mark. Usually I only needed to find the correct Hebrew equivalents to the Greek words in order to give good sense and understanding to the text. In other words, the syntax or word relationships were just such as one would expect in Hebrew.

All this was particularly surprising to me, for I remembered the problems I had as a student studying classical Greek in trying to juggle the words of Xenophon, Homer, Aeschylus, and Plato into the patterns of word order that English demands. What difficulty I had making those ancient Greeks speak English! And now, translating New Testament Greek into Hebrew, I was finding Greek written as if it were Hebrew.

Of course, there are many other indications of the Hebrew origin of our Gospel sources. I like to remember how a bright young Israeli student of mine gave me the clue to the meaning of the strange Greek word *ochloi* (''multitudes''). This word appears frequently in the Gospels; yet students and scholars alike have been puzzled because the translation, ''multitudes,'' seems rarely, if ever, to fit the context.

One day I mentioned in a lecture that I did not understand the odd use of *ochloi*, nor why it should appear in the plural. ''Ah,'' this young woman responded, ''that sounds exactly like the usage of the rabbis when they talk in the ancient writings of the people of a given place. Their word is *ochlosim*, a plural form, but which, of course, simply means 'the people of a locality.'''

Almost certainly this student was correct. In the story of the deliverance of a demonized man by Jesus, both Matthew and Luke say that when the demon emerged from the man ''the *ochloi* marveled.'' Clearly the meaning is not ''multitudes,'' but is, as we would say in English, ''those standing by.''

Even in the feeding of the five thousand, where both Matthew and Luke again combine to say that ''the *ochloi*" followed him, and where indeed there was a large crowd, it seemd better to translate Matthew 14:19 as "he commanded the people present to sit down," rather than "he commanded the *multitudes* to sit down." After all, it was just one multitude, not several. *Ochloi* is simply the literal Greek rendering of a Hebrew text which had *ochlosim* ("the people of the area"). This is only one of the hundreds of Hebraisms that lie hidden beneath the surface of the Greek texts of the Gospels of Matthew, Mark, and Luke.

The discovery that the first biography of Jesus was written in Hebrew, and the value of interpreting the words of Jesus through Hebrew, is in effect, the theme of David Bivin's and Roy Blizzard's book. They have accomplished a rare and difficult task in the writing of this book; that is, they have brought to light many of the "difficult words of Jesus" and opened up, to scholars and laymen alike, the wonders of his life and teachings. Surely all believers everywhere will welcome all the light available on Jesus, his language, and the Jewish setting which surrounded him. They will in no way be disappointed if they faithfully pursue the many clues presented within this work.

Robert L. Lindsey
Jerusalem, Israel

CHAPTER ONE

INTRODUCTION

It is indeed unfortunate that of all the New Testament writings, the words and sayings of Jesus himself are the most difficult to understand. Most Christians are unconsciously devoting the majority of their time in Bible study to the Epistles—almost completely ignoring the historical and Hebraic Synoptic Gospels (Matthew, Mark, and Luke). Without really understanding why, they tend to just "read over" the Synoptic Gospels. Phrases such as, "Blessed are the poor in spirit, for theirs is the kingdom of heaven," (Matthew 5:3)* sound so beautiful and poetic, but for the English speaker, do they convey any real depth of meaning?

Why are the words of Jesus that we find in the Synoptic Gospels so difficult to understand? The answer is that the original gospel that formed the basis for the Synoptic Gospels was first communicated, not in Greek, but in the Hebrew language. In spite of this, to-

*See pages 119-120 of the Appendix.

day's modern translations are all based upon a Greek text, derived from a still earlier Greek text, which is itself a translation of an original Hebrew *Life of Jesus*. This means that we are reading English translations of a text which is in itself a translation. Since the Synoptic Gospels are derived from an original Hebrew text, we are constantly "bumping into" Hebrew expressions or idioms which are often meaningless in Greek or in translations from the Greek.

The more Hebraic the saying or teaching of Jesus, the more difficult it is for us to understand. But it is just these Hebraic teachings that are often the strongest or most important. The difficulty arises because many of the sayings of Jesus are actually Hebrew idioms. An idiom is "an expression in the usage of a language, that is peculiar to itself either in grammatical construction or in having a meaning which cannot be derived as a whole from the conjoined meanings of its elements."* An example of an English idiom would be, "kill time," or, "hit the ceiling," or "eat your heart out." Many of the idioms that Jesus used in his teachings can be understood only when properly interpreted in a Hebrew context.

David Bivin relates his own experience as follows:

I began my Bible reading as a teenager. My greatest difficulty was trying to understand the words of Jesus. I would note sayings of Jesus such as "For if they do these things in a green tree, what shall be done in the dry?"

*Webster's New International Dictionary of the English Language (G. & C. Merriam Co.)

(Luke 23:31); * or, "From the days of John the Baptist until now, the kingdom of heaven suffereth violence, and the violent take it by force" (Matthew 11:12).**

Picture a teenager trying to make sense out of such good King James English as: "I am come to send fire on the earth; and what will I, if it be already kindled? But I have a baptism to be baptized with; and how am I straitened till it be accomplished!" (Luke 12:49-50).† I would question my pastor or teachers or visiting seminary professors as to the meaning of such passages and would invariably receive the common response, "Just keep reading, son, the Bible will interpret itself."

The truth is that one can keep reading the Bible until the day he dies and the Bible will not tell him the meaning of these difficult Hebrew passages. They can be understood only when translated back into Hebrew. What my pastor and teachers should have admonished was, "Son, learn Hebrew! These are all Hebrew expressions or idioms that can be understood only if you know Hebrew."

These men of God I questioned could not help me; however, they cannot be blamed for lack of an answer. No one had ever suggested

---

*See pages 120-123 of the Appendix.
**See pages 123-125 of the Appendix.
† See pages 126-142 of the Appendix.

to them that the most important tool for understanding the Bible—both Old and New Testaments—is Hebrew, and that Hebrew is the key to understanding the words of Jesus.

By the time I went to Israel at the age of 24 to study at the Hebrew University, I had almost stopped reading the Gospels. It wasn't that I wasn't reading the Bible. I was reading the Bible more than ever before, but I was unconsciously neglecting the Gospels; yet, here were the real words and teachings of Jesus.

Our reasons for writing this book are not only to show that the original gospel was communicated in the Hebrew language; but to show that the entire New Testament can only be understood from a Hebrew perspective.

Most Christians are aware that the Old Testament was originally communicated in Hebrew, and that it is important to know Hebrew to understand the Old Testament. What they do not recognize, however, is the importance of Hebrew in understanding the New Testament.

It should be emphasized that the Bible (both Old *and* New Testaments) is, in its entirety, highly Hebraic. In spite of the fact that portions of the New Testament were communicated in Greek, the background is thoroughly Hebrew. The writers are Hebrew, the culture is Hebrew, the religion is Hebrew, the traditions are Hebrew, and the concepts are Hebrew.

We tend to forget that the Old Testament comprises approximately 78% of the biblical text, and the New Testament only 22%. When we add the highly Hebraic portions of the New Testament (Matthew, Mark, Luke, and Acts 1:1 – 15:35,* approximately 43% of the New Testament) to the Old Testament, the percentage of biblical material originally written in Hebrew rises to 88% (or 87% if we omit the portions of Ezra and Daniel — less than 1% of the Old Testament — composed in Aramaic). Not more than 12% of the entire Bible was originally written in Greek. When we subtract from that 12% the 176 quotations from the Old Testament (14 Old Testament quotations in John and 162 from Acts 15:36 to the end of the New Testament), the percentage of the Bible originally composed in Hebrew rises to over 90%.

The assumption that the entire New Testament was originally communicated in Greek has led to a considerable amount of misunderstanding on the part of scholars and layman alike. Today, as a result of recent research, we know that the key to our understanding of this material is Hebrew. To this present day there has been in New Testament studies a disproportionate stress placed on the study of Greek and Hellenism. If any additional advances are to be made, especially in better understanding the words of Jesus, the concentration must shift to the study of Hebrew history and culture, and above all, the Hebrew language.

---

*The first 15 chapters of Acts show some of the same textual evidence as the Synoptic Gospels of being originally communicated in Hebrew. They deal with events in Jerusalem and are recounted in a Hebrew context. In Acts 15:36 there is a historical shift to the Greek context of Paul's missionary journeys.

CHAPTER TWO

THE ASSUMPTIONS OF LIBERAL SCHOLARSHIP

There are many different theories and variations of theories as to the origins of the Synoptic Gospels and the language in which they were originally communicated. The problem of the relationship of the Synoptists was first seriously discussed by Augustine (d. 430 A.D.). The most commonly accepted theory today is that Mark was the first of the Synoptic Gospels, and that Matthew and Luke used Mark in writing their Gospels. The originality and priority of Mark was first suggested in the late eighteenth century and remains the prevailing theory among most New Testament critics. In addition, most scholars, for the last 150-200 years, have generally assumed either a Greek or Aramaic origin for the Synoptic material.

These basic assumptions of scholarship have in many ways proved to be a hinderance in establishing a proper approach to biblical study. For example, the New Testament records of the life of Jesus and all his teachings were alleged by liberal scholars to be based on late, faulty transmission of oral reports recorded by a Greek-speaking Church far removed from the unsophisticated Judean and Galilean scene. This liberal scholarship greatly influenced the evangelical approach to the New Testament. Evangelicals, who were often less formally educated, and thus unable to critically appraise the assumptions of liberal scholarship, surprisingly fell right into line. One recent (1974) survey of the New Testament by Robert G. Gromacki, an evangelical, contains the following statements:

> Although Alexander is mainly known as a great military strategist, his main contribution was in spreading the Greek culture and language to the Near East. The Hellenization was so complete that the next six hundred years (300 B.C. – A.D. 300) saw Greek become the lingua franca of the Mediterranean world. A highly sophisticated language with its many declensions, conjugations, and grammatical technicalities, it was the perfect medium in which the New Testament could be written (Gromacki 1974:7).

Note the assumption that the original language of the whole of the New Testament is Greek. In another place, Gromacki states:

> As someone has pointed out [Gromacki does not specify the source], the Greek text of Matthew reads more like an original edition than like a translation. Harrison correctly observes: ''Despite this tradition of a Semitic original, the Fathers have no information on the translation of it into Greek. What they

knew and used for themselves was a Greek Gospel." The statement by Papias is intriguing, but until more objective evidence is forthcoming, the position that Matthew wrote the entire book in Greek must stand (Gromacki 1974:7).

To say that the statement of Papias, a church father of the second century, is "intriguing" is to question Papias' verasity. The simple, straightforward statement of Papias seems objective enough: "Matthew put down the words of the Lord in the Hebrew language, and others have translated them each as best he could" (Eusebius, *Ecclesiastical History* III 39, 16).*

Scholarly assumptions as to the linguistic origins of the Synoptic Gospels have become so deeply ingrained in the thinking of most non-Hebrew speaking Christians that to challenge these hypotheses is considered by most as near heresy. Be that as it may, it can be stated unequivocally that the original *Life of Jesus* was communicated in Hebrew; and that Hebrew was also, very likely, the spoken language of Jesus of Nazareth. This being the case, it necessitates an entire reexamination of the popular theories about linguistic origins and a reorientation in the study of the New Testament.

*See also page 46.

CHAPTER THREE

AN EXAMINATION OF THE
ARAMAIC AND GREEK THEORIES

In view of the fact that the majority of New Testament scholars have in recent times favored an Aramaic or Greek origin for the Synoptic Gospels, it is necessary for us to examine the pros and cons of these two theories.

THE ARAMAIC THEORY

It is interesting that the same individuals who espouse the inerrancy of the Scriptures will take the specific passages in the New Testament that refer to Jesus speaking Hebrew (Acts 26:14), or Paul speaking He - brew (Acts 21:40), and say, "That means Aramaic, and not Hebrew."

The "Aramaic Theory" has so heavily influenced biblical scholarship that even those who should be the most capable of working with the biblical text, namely, Bible translators, have translated "Aramaic" when the original text specifically states "Hebrew." For example, the New International Version, published by Zondervan Bible Publishers, in both of the above mentioned passages in Acts, purposely translates "Hebrew" as "Aramaic," and only in 26:14 does it even bother to give the footnote "or Hebrew" in italics at the bottom of the page. The New American Standard Bible translates "Hebrew dialect" in both passages, but adds the footnote, "i.e., Jewish Aramaic."

Since the majority of scholars have favored Aramaic origins for the Synoptic Gospels, there must be strong reasons for their acceptance of this theory. But, when one examines the evidence, one learns that there are no strong reasons available to support an Aramaic origin apart from the appearance of certain Aramaic, or what often seem to be Aramaic, words or phrases scattered through the New Testament text, particularly the text of the Gospels. In fact, there is much stronger evidence against the theory of Aramaic origins.*

According to Codex Sinaiticus, Codex Alexandrinus, and Codex Bezae, three of the most ancient Greek manuscripts of the New Testament, dating from the fourth and fifth centuries A.D., it is stated that the inscription "This is the King of Jews" (Luke 23:38) over the cross of Jesus was written in "Greek, Latin, and Hebrew letters." Is it not significant that the oldest Greek textual tradition infers that Hebrew was more popular than Aramaic in this period?

Those who claim an Aramaic cultural milieu for that period have often noted that our Gospels contain Aramaic words like *"Talitha cumi," "Ephphata,"*

---

*See pages 54-55 for a short history of the Aramaic language.

"*Rabboni*," and a few others. Although it is true that our Gospels do have some Aramaic words, so do all the Hebrew documents written around the time of Jesus — for instance, the Mishnah and the Dead Sea Scrolls. The Book of Jeremiah, dating from a much earlier period and overwhelmingly Hebrew, includes a sentence in Aramaic (Jeremiah 10:11). Even the Book of Genesis contains a two-word Aramaic phrase (Genesis 31:47).*

In the Hebrew of the first century we find many Aramaic loan words, i.e., words borrowed from Aramaic. This is also true of the New Testament; however, upon closer scrutiny, many supposed Aramaic words turn out to be Hebrew. For instance, *sikera* (strong drink, Luke 1:15), is always included in lists of the Aramaic words of the New Testament. Because of the ending "*a*," it is assumed that *sikera* is a Greek transliteration of the Aramaic *shikra*, rather than the Hebrew *sheichar*. However, if one will check in *Hatch-Redpath's Concordance to the Septuagint*,** he will note that *sikera* is the standard Greek translation of the Hebrew *sheichar*. The "*a*" ending is not the Aramaic definite article, but simply the Greek neuter ending. What is true of the "*a*" in *sikera* is also true of the "*a*" in *Sabbata* (Matthew 12:10) and *Pascha* (Passover, Luke 2:41).

Even the presence of an Aramaic word, such as

*We have previously noted (page 23) that portions of Ezra and Daniel (Ezra 4:8-6:18, 7:12-26; Daniel 2:4-7:28), less than 1% of the Old Testament, were composed in Aramaic.

**See Bibliography, page 171. (The Septuagint is the Greek translation of the Old Testament, from the second century B.C.)

Abba (Mark 14:36), does not prove the existence of an Aramaic original. *Abba* appears over and over in the Hebrew writings of the period as a loan word, borrowed from Aramaic because of its special flavor and used in the same way as we use "daddy" or "papa" in English. Today, in modern Israel, children use *Abba* in addressing their fathers, exactly the same way as it was used in the time of Jesus.

Perhaps the most often quoted Aramaism in the New Testament is the sentence in Mark 15:34, *"Eloi, Eloi, lama sabakthani."* These words are Aramaic, but it is doubtful that Jesus spoke them as Mark records—the people hearing the words thought Jesus was calling Elijah. For them to make such a mistake, Jesus would have to have cried, *"Eli, Eli,"* not *"Eloi, Eloi."* Why? Because *Eli* in Hebrew can be either "My God," or a shortened form of *Eliyahu*, Hebrew for Elijah. But the Aramaic *Eloi* can be only "My God." One must note that Matthew's account records just that, i.e., *"Eli, Eli"* (Matthew 27:46). Further, *lama* ("why") is the same word in both languages, and *sabak* is a verb which is found not only in Aramaic, but also in Mishnaic Hebrew.

On the basis of the few Aramaic words that might be found, should we overlook the many more numerous Hebrew words that appear in the Greek text of the Gospels, such as: *levonah* (frankincense, Matthew 2:11), *mammon* (Luke 16:9), *Wai* (Woe! Matthew 23:13), *rabbi* (Matthew 23:7,8), *Beelzebub* (Luke 11:15), *corban* (Mark 7:11), *Satan* (Luke 10:18), *cammon* (cummin, Matthew 23:23), *raca* (a term of contempt; literally, "empty," Matthew 5:22), *moreh* (rebel,

Matthew 5:22), *bath* (a wet measure, between 8-9 gallons, Luke 16:6), *kor* (a dry measure, between 10-12 bushels, Luke 16:7), *zuneem* (tares, Matthew 13:25), *Boanerges* (Mark 3:17), *mor* (myrrh, Luke 7:37), *sheekmah* (sycamore, Luke 12:5), and *amen,* which appears about 100 times in the Greek text of the Gospels.

Today, the evidence for Hebrew is quite overwhelming; and yet, many Christians still cling to the outmoded Aramaic hypothesis as if their faith depended upon it. Over the years, whenever any scholar argued in favor of Hebrew or when Hebrew scrolls or inscriptions came to light, advocates of the Aramaic theory were quick to explain away the evidence. For example:

1. When the New Testament or Josephus says, ''Hebrew,'' proponents of the Aramaic hypothesis say, ''What is meant is 'Aramaic.' ''

2. When only Hebrew, Greek, and a few Latin inscriptions were found from the Roman period in the Temple Mount excavations, it was said of the Hebrew inscriptions, ''They are only representative of the Hebrew used by the priests in the sacred area, but not indicative of the spoken language of the common man.''

3. It was said of the Mishnah and other rabbinic works, ''These admittedly are written in Hebrew, but it is an artificial language used only for study and discussion by the Rabbis and their students in the Talmudic academies.''

Concerning this last argument, it should be noted that as early as 1927 the great Jewish scholar, M. H. Segal, demonstrated conclusively that Mishnaic Hebrew was not an artificial language used only by rabbinic scholars in Talmudic academies, but that it exhibits all the characteristics of a living language.*

The authors do not wish to imply that Aramaic, as well as Greek, were not spoken in Israel in the first centuries B.C.–A.D. Certainly most of the people were multilingual, or at least bilingual, with Aramaic, Greek, and even some Latin in common use alongside of Hebrew. To quote Segal:

> ...what was the language of ordinary life of educated native Jews in Jerusalem and Judea in the period from 400 B.C. to 150 A.D.? The evidence presented by Mishnaic Hebrew and its literature leaves no doubt that that language was Mishnaic Hebrew. Of course, those educated Judeans also understood Aramaic, and used it even in writing, but only occasionally, and not habitually—in the same way as...the Flamand in Belgium may often use French (Segal 1927:13).

Segal's conclusions were largely ignored by Christian scholars and soon forgotten.

Since the discovery of the Dead Sea Scrolls, however, the leading proponents of the Aramaic theory have gradually begun to modify their views. Matthew Black, for instance, in the third edition[**] of his influential book, *An Aramaic Approach to the Gospels and Acts*, remarks:

---

*In fact, Segal first put forward his views in 1909 in an article which appeared in the *Jewish Quarterly Review*, Volume XX, pages 647-737.

** The second edition of Black's book was written before the Qumran texts became available to scholars.

The Qumran discoveries have also shed fresh light on the problem: M. Wilcox writes: "With regard to the matter of language, we ought to note that the discovery of the Dead Sea Scrolls has now placed at our disposal information of a highly interesting and relevant nature...The non-Biblical texts show us a free, living language, and attest the fact that in New Testament times, and for some considerable time previously, Hebrew was not confined to Rabbinical circles by any means, but appeared as a normal vehicle of expression."*

Fig. 1. The column of the Isaiah Scroll from Cave I at Qumran, containing Isaiah 40:3 (beginning in the middle of line 2). The Isaiah Scroll is the best preserved of the almost 600 manuscripts that have been found in the eleven Qumran caves. (Courtesy of the Shrine of the Book, Israel Museum.)

*Max Wilcox is one of the many students of Professor Black. The quotation is from Wilcox's *The Semitisms of Acts* (1965), page 14.

. . . If this is a correct estimate of the Qumran evidence, where Hebrew certainly vastly predominates over Aramaic, then it may be held to confirm the view identified with the name of Professor Segal that Hebrew was actually a spoken vernacular in Judaea in the time of Christ (Black 1967: 47).

It cannot be ignored when discussing the linguistic milieu of first-century Palestine that the foremost Aramaic theorist, Matthew Black, is now obliged to admit: ''We must nevertheless allow possibly more than has been done before for the use of Hebrew in addition to (or instead of) Aramaic by Jesus Himself. . .'' (Black 1967: 49).

THE GREEK THEORY

Although the overwhelming majority of scholars subscribe to a Semitic origin for the Gospels, there are those, none the less, such as the English scholar Nigel Turner,* who propose a Greek origin. Apart from linguistic and cultural arguments for Semitic origins, it remains an important fact that the poor Greek of the Synoptic Gospels is found basically only in literary works that are translations from Semitic originals, such as the Septuagint.

Many Gospel expressions are not just poor Greek, but actually meaningless in Greek. One brief example will suffice to illustrate this fact. The text of Matthew 6:22-23 literally reads: ''The lamp of the body is the eye. If your eye is good, your whole body is full of light;

*See Bibliography, page 172.

but if your eye is bad your whole body is full of darkness..." The expressions "good eye"* and "bad eye" are common Hebrew idioms for "generous" and "miserly." Greek has no such idioms, and in Greek this statement of Jesus is meaningless, just as it is in English.

Why is the Greek of the Gospels such poor Greek? Very simply, because the Gospels of Matthew, Mark, and Luke are not really Greek, but Hebrew words in Greek dress, or, we might say, "translation" Greek. Are we claiming that the Synoptic Gospels were not originally written in Greek? To this we must answer yes and no. The Synoptic Gospels as we have them today were originally written in Greek; however, the text from which they descend was originally translated from a Hebrew archetype.**

It is easy to see how scholars such as Gromacki and Turner, not understanding this process of Gospel textual transmission, could assume a Greek text. However, it is the undertext of our canonical Gospels that reveals the Hebrew original. † Our canonical Gospels are based on Greek texts derived from the Greek translation of the original Hebrew story of the life of Jesus.

It is most unfortunate that our Bible colleges and seminaries focus their attention on Greek and Hellenistic theology, and fail by and large to equip their students with the proper tools that would allow them to do serious biblical exegesis. A strong statement, to be sure; but sadly, all too true. *It cannot be overemphasized*, that the key to an understanding of the New Testament is a fluent

---

*See the discussion of "good eye" on pages 144-145 of the Appendix.
**See pages 94-98 for a discussion of the process of textual transmission.
†See Chapter 6 for a more detailed discussion of the evidences for the Hebrew undertext.

knowledge of Hebrew and an intimate acquaintance with Jewish history, culture, and Rabbinic Literature.

The evidence for Aramaic or Greek origins of the Synoptic Gospels simply will not stand up under critical analysis. There is far more substantial evidence indicating a Hebrew origin of the Synoptic Gospels.

CHAPTER FOUR

RECENT LINGUISTIC RESEARCH

A revolution is taking place in our understanding of the New Testament. With the rebirth of Israel in 1947-1948 came the dramatic discovery of the Dead Sea Scrolls. These priceless, ancient manuscripts, followed a few years later by the discovery of the Bar-Cochba letters, became vital contributions to a fuller understanding of the New Testament writings.

Many scholars in Israel are now convinced that the spoken and written language of the Jews in the Land of Israel at the time of Jesus was indeed Hebrew; and that the Synoptic Gospels were derived from original Hebrew sources.

These scholars, fluent in both Greek and Hebrew, have proposed impressive solutions to major problems of New Testament interpretation. Important discoveries which they have made serve to illuminate the very Hebraic style of speech used by Jesus and his first followers, and to make possible a more accurate translation of the Gospels. With a new understanding of the language Jesus spoke, they are now able to correct numerous mistranslations in the English text of the New Testament.

The late Jehoshua M. Grintz wrote an article entitled ''Hebrew as the Spoken and Written Language in the Last Days of the Second Temple'' (Grintz 1960). On the basis of his study of Matthew's Gospel and other literature contemporary with the Gospels, Grintz asserted that ''Hebrew was the only literary language of that time; and to this alone we can attribute the fact that the new sect of 'unlearned and ignorant men' (Acts 4:13) set out to write its main book, intended for its Jewish members, in this language'' (Grintz 1960: 46). Grintz further emphasizes: ''Moreover, Hebrew was then the main vehicle of *speech* [emphasis the authors'] in Jewish Palestine, or at least in Jerusalem and Judea.'' He provides evidence for this statement with a relevant story, narrated in the Talmud (Nedarim 66b) about the difficulties an Aramaic-speaking Jew from Babylon had in communicating with his Jerusalemite wife (Grintz 1960: 46-47).

Professor David Flusser, of the Hebrew University of Jerusalem, and the world's leading Jewish authority on the New Testament and early Christianity, holds strongly to the view that the *Life of Jesus* was originally composed in Hebrew. He claims there are hundreds of Semitisms (Semitic idioms) in the Synoptic Gospels which could only be Hebrew, but there are no Semitisms which could only be Aramaic without also being good Hebrew.

Dr. Moshe Bar-Asher, who has inherited the late Professor Yehezkiel Kutscher's reputation as the foremost Aramaic scholar at the Hebrew University, says that he believes the Synoptic Gospels go back to a Greek translation of an original Hebrew (not Aramaic!) document.

Dr. Pinhas Lapide, Director of the School for Translators and Interpreters at Bar-Ilan University in Tel Aviv, has written an article entitled "The Missing Hebrew Gospel"(Lapide 1974). In this article he discusses the Hebrew origins of the Gospels. Dr. Lapide, a scholar fluent in more than a dozen languages, states:

> No less significant is the fact, borne out by subsequent documentary finds at Murabba'at, Nahal Heber, and on Masada, that, throughout the first Christian century (and later), religious topics were mainly recorded in Hebrew (Lapide 1974:   169).

Dr. Lapide concludes:

> The past century has witnessed the unexpected discovery of such literary treasure-troves as in the Cairo Geniza and the Qumran

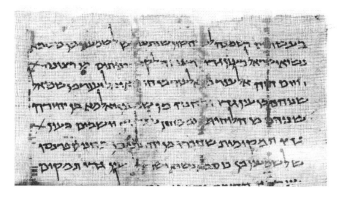

Fig. 2. A Hebrew deed written on papyrus found in Nahal Hever. It begins: "On the 28th of Marheshvan, the third year of Shimon ben Kosiba, [Hebrew, "son of"] Kosiba, President of Israel; at En-gedi." (See Yadin's *Bar Kokhba*, p. 177) (Courtesy of the Shrine of the Book, Israel Museum. Photo: David Harris)

and Murabba'at caves. It is not impossible than an excavator may yet unearth a fragment of that earliest Hebrew Gospel 'according to the Jews' (Lapide 1974: 170).

Outstanding scholars from outside Israel have also arrived at the conclusion that the language of Jesus was Hebrew. One such scholar is Harris Birkeland, a Norwegian. In his article entitled "The Language of Jesus," Birkeland challenges the current view that the language of Jesus was Aramaic. His conclusion is: "The language of the common people in Palestine in the time of Jesus was Hebrew." He continues: "My further conclusion...that Jesus really used Hebrew, also seems unavoidable" (Birkeland 1954: 39).

William Sanford LaSor, professor emeritus at Fuller Theological Seminary, is an outstanding Semitic scholar. In a recent lecture delivered in Jerusalem, April 24, 1982, he stated:

> With the discovery of the Dead Sea Scrolls, it now seems highly probable that the language Jesus spoke was Hebrew and not Aramaic The sectarians at Qumran not only wrote their commentaries on books of the Bible in Hebrew, but their manual for new members and books regulating the life of the community, such as the *Manual of Discipline* and the *Damascus Covenant*, were also written in Hebrew.

Professor Frank Cross, of Harvard University, is probably the leading living authority on the handwriting of the Dead Sea Scrolls. Professor Cross has stated that by observing the handwriting of the various scribes who copied the scrolls over the centuries at Qumran, it can be seen that the dominant language of Palestine beginning about 130 B.C. was Hebrew. By studying the mistakes in copying made by the scribes of Qumran, Cross determined that they had an inferior knowledge of Aramaic grammar and syntax, and that their principal language was Hebrew.

Another brilliant scholar is M. L'Abbe' J. T. Milik. Milik, a Polish priest, is well-known in scientific and archaeological circles. He was one of the excavators of Qumran and the most active member of the international team which prepared the scrolls from Cave IV for publication. After a careful analysis of all the textual materials from the Judean Desert, Milik concluded:

> The copper rolls and documents from the Second Revolt prove beyond reasonable doubt that Mishnaic [Hebrew] was the normal language of the Judean population in the Roman Period (Milik 1963: 130).

The conclusions of the above scholars carry all the more weight when coupled with examples from extrabiblical sources and from the Gospels themselves presented in the following chapters.

CHAPTER FIVE

EXTRA-BIBLICAL EVIDENCE FOR HEBREW

An impressive amount of extra-biblical evidence
points to the use of Hebrew in first-century Israel: the
testimony of the church fathers, the Dead Sea Scrolls,
coins and inscriptions from the first centuries B.C.
– A.D., the writings of Josephus, and Rabbinic Literature. In this chapter we will examine some of that
evidence.

THE CHURCH FATHERS

The early church fathers are usually referred to as
the Ante-Nicean Fathers, i.e., the leaders of the primitive Christian Church up to the Council of Nicea in approximately 325 A.D. Their testimony is important because it carries us back to the early centuries of the
Christian Era.

The evidence provided by the early church fathers
contradicts the theory of an Aramaic origin of the Gospels. (Actually, the Aramaic theory is a relatively late

development—dating probably no earlier than the Middle Ages.) Our earliest witness is Papias, Bishop of Hierapolis, in Asia Minor (mid-second century A.D.). Concerning the Hebrew origin of the Gospels, he states:

> Matthew put down the words of the Lord in the Hebrew language, and others have translated them, each as best he could (Eusebius, *Ecclesiastical History* III 39, 16).

Irenaeus (120-202 A.D.) was Bishop of Lyons, in France. Most of his literary endeavors were undertaken in the last quarter of the second century A.D. Irenaeus states:

> Matthew, indeed, produced his Gospel written among the Hebrews in their own dialect (Eusebius, *Ecclesiastical History* V 8, 2).

Origen (first quarter of the third century), in his commentary on Matthew, states:

> The first [Gospel], composed in the Hebrew language, was written by Matthew...for those who came to faith from Judaism (Eusebius, *Ecclesiastical History* VI 25, 4).

Eusebius, Bishop of Caesarea (circa 325 A.D.), writes:

> Matthew had first preached to the Hebrews, and when he was about to go to others also, he transmitted his Gospel in writing in his native language *(Ecclesiastical History* III 24, 6).

These are but a few of the references in the writings of the early church fathers that indicate a Hebrew origin for the Gospels. In addition to these, there are many references in the later church fathers (the Post-Nicean

Fathers, from approximately 325 A.D.). Epiphanius,*
for instance, writes at length about the Jewish-Christian
sect of the Nazarenes:

> They have the entire Gospel of Matthew in
> Hebrew. It is carefully preserved by them as it
> was originally written, in Hebrew script
> (*Refutation of All Heresies* 29, 9, 4).

Epiphanius also writes about the Ebionites, another
messianic sect:

> And they too accept the Gospel of Matthew
> ...they call it "according to the Hebrews,"
> and that is the correct way of speaking since
> Matthew alone of the New Testament writers
> presents the gospel in Hebrew and in the He-
> brew script (*Refutation of All Heresies* 30,3,
> 7).

Jerome** was by far the most knowledgeable in Hebrew of all the church fathers. His Latin translation of
the Bible, the Vulgate, has remained until today the au-
thoritative Bible of the Roman Catholic Church. Jerome
lived the last 31 years of his life in Bethlehem. It was
there that he produced his Latin translation of the Old
Testament, made directly from the Hebrew. Concerning
Matthew's Gospel, Jerome writes:

> Matthew was the first in Judea to compose the
> gospel of Christ in Hebrew letters and words
> ...Who it was that later translated it into
> Greek is no longer known with certainty. Fur-
> thermore, the Hebrew text itself is still pre-
> served in the library at Caesarea which the

---

*Died 403 A.D.
**Died 420 A.D.

martyr Pamphilus assembled with great care
(*De Viris Inlustribus* 3).

Further evidence for the Hebrew origin of the Gospels is mentioned by Lapide:

A recently published Arabic polemic seems to refute once and for all the views of those few scholars who still wish to write off all Patristic references to "Hebrew" as mere mistakes for Aramaic. The manuscript, composed in the tenth century, is partly based upon an Aramaic document of the fifth century... The text, which repeatedly dwells on the importance of Hebrew (al-ibranniyya), "the language of Jesus and the Prophets," in which "the true Gospel" had been composed, reproaches the (Gentile) Christians for "having abandoned this language," instead of which they took up numerous other languages which had not been spoken by Jesus and his companions" (Lapide 1974: 168).*

If, in spite of the above evidence, one should still wish to brush aside the witness of the church fathers as mere "tradition," one final fact must be noted. There exists no early church tradition whatsoever for a primitive Aramaic gospel.

THE DEAD SEA SCROLLS

The Dead Sea Scrolls represent a portion of the library from the Jewish community at Qumran, a small

*Lapide is referring to the Arabic document published by Shlomo Pines (See Bibliography, page 172).

site located on the northwestern shore of the Dead Sea. In 68 A.D., two years after the outbreak of the Jewish Revolt in Jerusalem, the community met an untimely end when Qumran was attacked and destroyed by the Roman army.

The Dead Sea Scrolls are the most dramatic and significant archaeological discovery of all times relating to the biblical text. The finds were brought to light over a 16-year period from 1947 to 1963 (when additional scroll finds were made at Masada). They include close to 600 partial manuscripts (biblical and non-biblical) indicated by some 40,000 fragments. One hundred and seventy-nine Old Testament manuscripts (many very fragmentary), representing every book except Esther, have been found. These finds provide us with Hebrew manuscripts of the Bible over 1,000 years older than any previously known, some only a few hundred years removed from the original "autographs."

Members of the Dead Sea community, in addition to copying biblical manuscripts, also wrote many original books, such as manuals for new initiates, intended for members of their community. Of the ten major non-biblical scrolls published to date, *only one,* the Genesis Apocryphon, is in Aramaic. The most recently published scroll, and the longest to date (28 feet, equivalent to over 80 Old Testament chapters), is the now-famous Temple Scroll,* also written in Hebrew.

These sectarian scrolls are significant in the discussion of the literary language of the first centuries B.C. – A.D. since they are not simply copies of biblical texts composed hundreds of years earlier, but entirely

*See Bibliography, page 172.

Fig. 3. Four columns of the Temple Scroll. (Courtesy of the Shrine of the Book, Israel Museum. Photo: David Harris)

composed in a period contemporary with Jesus.

Scholars have only just begun to study and to appreciate this vast literature. The number of New Testament parallels found in these texts is truly remarkable. The following is an interesting example of such a parallel. Note the similarity to Galatians 5:16-26:

> ...the God of Israel and His Angel of Truth have helped all the sons of light. It is He who created the spirits of light and darkness...and these are their ways in the world: to enlighten the heart of man, to make straight before him all the ways of true righteousness, to instill in his heart a fear of the judgments of God, a spirit of humility, patience, abundant compassion, eternal goodness, understanding, insight and mighty wisdom which is founded on all the works of God and leans on His abundant loving-kindness, a spirit of discernment in every purpose, zeal for righteous judg-

ments, holy intent with steadfastness of heart, great love for all the sons of truth, virtuous purity which abhors all defilement of idols, modesty of behavior with prudence in all things and faithfulness in concealing the mysteries of knowledge—these are the counsels of the spirit to the sons of truth in this world. And the reward of all who walk in its ways is healing, a long and peaceful life, and fruitfulness together with every eternal blessing and unending joy in life everlasting, a crown of glory and a garment of majesty amid unending light.

But to the spirit of perversity belong greed, slackness in the service of righteousness, wickedness and lies, pride and haughtiness, denial and deceit, cruelty and great hypocrisy, shortness of temper and profusion

Fig. 4. The Manual of Discipline (Columns I-IV). (Courtesy of the Shrine of the Book, Israel Museum. Photo: David Harris)

of folly, brazen insolence, abominable deeds (committed) in a spirit of fornication, filthy ways in the service of uncleanness, a blaspheming tongue, blindess of eye and dullness of ear, stiffness of neck and hardness of heart, so that a man walks entirely in the ways of darkness and guile. And the reward of all who walk in its ways is a multitude of afflictions at the hands of all the angels of destruction, eternal damnation through the angry wrath of an avenging God, eternal trembling, everlasting dishonor with endless disgrace in the fire of dark places. The times of all their generations will be spent in sorrowful mourning, bitter misfortune, calamities of darkness until they are destroyed without remnant or survivor (Manual of Discipline III 24–IV 14).

If we compare the total number of pages in these ten sectarian scrolls we again find a nine-to-one ratio of Hebrew to Aramaic (179 pages in the nine Hebrew scrolls, to 22 pages of Aramaic in the Genesis Apocryphon). It is even possible that the Genesis Apocryphon was not originally written by the Qumran sectarians contemporary with Jesus, but is a Targum (see definition below) originally written a century or two earlier when Aramaic was more popular.

Advocates of the Aramaic theory are quick to point out the presence of Targums among the manuscripts discovered in the Dead Sea caves. (A Targum is an Aramaic translation of Scripture, often expanded to include explanations and comments.) A Targum of Job was discovered in Cave 11, and a Targum of Leviticus in Cave 4. It is assumed that the existence of Targums is evidence for the need of the common folk for a version of the Scriptures in a language they could more easily understand, namely Aramaic.* (It is interesting to note that even before the discovery of the Targum of Job at Qumran, we knew of its existence. We are told in the Talmud, in *Shabbath* 115a, that a Targum of Job was once brought to Gamaliel, the teacher of Paul. He ordered it to be built into the walls of the Temple, which at that time were still under construction.)

What the advocates of the Aramaic theory neglect to point out is that Greek translations of Scripture at Qumran outnumber the Targums (Aramaic translations). To date, Greek translations of Exodus, Leviticus, and Numbers have been discovered at Qumran. If the existence of Aramaic translations of Scripture in the first century could prove the common people spoke Aramaic, then the existence of Greek translations of Scripture could just as surely prove they spoke Greek. However, no one argues that Greek was the spoken language of first-century Israel!

Advocates of Aramaic also fail to recognize the significance of the numerous *Pesharim* (commentaries) found at Qumran. *Pesharim* exist on Isaiah, Hosea, Micah, Nahum, Habakkuk, Zephaniah, Psalms, and on scattered passages from other books of the Old Testament. All of the *Pesharim* are written in Hebrew. Is it feasible that commentary on Scripture was written in a language that the majority of the people did not understand? Certainly not, since the study of Scripture was

---

*A more probable explanation for the existence of Targums is that they performed a useful service for the bilingual and multilingual residents of the Land of Israel — the Aramaic translation interpreted the Hebrew text. For religious reasons, the Hebrew original could not be even slightly altered or expanded, but its Aramaic translation could, wherever necessary, comment on and explain hard-to-understand passages.

Fig. 5. The Habakkuk Pesher (Commentary) Columns IX-XII.
(Courtesy of the Shrine of the Book, Israel Museum. Photo:
David Harris)

not in Judaism the prerogative of a priestly caste.

As was mentioned earlier (pages 42-43), Professor Frank Cross has concluded that Hebrew had replaced Aramaic and was the most commonly used language in Palestine by 130 B.C. An interesting question is why?

Like Hebrew, Aramaic belongs to the Semitic family of languages. Many words are common to both languages; still other words have the same root. Aramaic was the official language of Persia as well as being the *lingua franca* of Assyria and Babylon from 700–300 B.C. The influence of Aramaic upon the Kingdoms of Judah and Samaria was considerable; although its influence in the Northern Kingdom was greater than in Judah, as the Northern Kingdom of Samaria was conquered by Assyria 134 years before the defeat of Judah.

When a large part of the population of the Southern Kingdom of Judah was carried away into Babylonian captivity in 587 B.C., numerous changes took place. Aramaic was adopted by most of the Jews in captivity. When the Jews were allowed to return in 538 B.C., they had become so accustomed to life in Babylon that only 40,000 returned to Jerusalem. Most of those returning used Aramaic as their principal language, while the Jews who had not been exiled and who had remained in Judah still spoke Hebrew. The inhabitants of Judah soon developed a multilingual culture and probably used Hebrew and Aramaic almost equally.

In 167 B.C., the Temple was desecrated by Antiochus IV Epiphanes, the Syrian Selucid ruler over Palestine. Shortly thereafter, the Jews, led by Judas Maccabaeus, revolted against the tyranny and harsh policies of Antiochus. There seems little doubt that this revolt, which culminated in the cleansing of the Temple in December of 164 B.C., spurred a religious revival among the Jews. It was the Maccabean victory which gradually led to a reinstatement of the ancestral language, Hebrew, as the dominant language in the whole of Palestine. Similarly, in recent times, it was Hebrew that won the struggle over which language would be the national language of the Jews living once again in their homeland, later to become the modern-day State of Israel.

COINS AND INSCRIPTIONS

The evidence provided by coins is also important in trying to evaluate the linguistic situation in the time of Jesus. Ya'akov Meshorer, Curator of the Numismatic Department of the Israel Museum, and its numismatic expert, has listed 215 Jewish coins in his catalogue.* Of these, 99 have Hebrew inscriptions—only one has an Aramaic inscription!**From the fourth century B.C. (late Persian Period) until the end of the Bar-Cochba

*See Bibliography, page 172.

** The coins inscribed in Greek are even more numerous than those inscribed

OBVERSE REVERSE

Fig. 6. **Bronze Coin minted by Alexander Jannaeus.**
Obverse: An anchor encircled by the Greek inscription, "Of King Alexander." Reverse: A star with eight rays. Around the star, the Aramaic letters spelling "The King Alexandros, Year 25."

Fig. 7. **Bronze coin minted by Herod the Great in the third year of his reign (See Meshorer, coin 39).**
Obverse: Greek inscription: "Of King Herod." Reverse: Pomegranate with branch.

Fig. 8. **Bronze coin minted during the Bar-Cochba Revolt (See Meshorer, Coin 191).**
Obverse: Inscription "Jerusalem" within a wreath. Reverse: An amphora with the Hebrew letters "shblchr (year two of the freedom of) Israel."

Fig. 9. **Silver shekel minted in 66 A.D. during the Great Jewish Revolt against Rome (See Meshorer, Coin 148).**
Obverse only: Chalice with the Hebrew letter aleph (year one) with the inscription "shekel of Israel."

All coins enlarged 2.5x. All photographs courtesy of the Israel Museum.

Revolt in 135 A.D., the entire history of Jewish coin-age, only one Jewish coin, minted during the reign of Alexander Jannaeus (103–76 B.C.), is inscribed in Aramaic.

In addition to the evidence from coins, there is a considerable epigraphical evidence from inscriptions. The archaeological excavations at the Temple Mount, directed by Professor Benjamin Mazar of the Hebrew

Fig. 10. Aerial view of the archaeological excavations at the Temple Mount.

in Hebrew; however, the Greek coins come almost entirely from the time of the Roman quisling, Herod, and his heirs. All the coins minted by Herod and his descendants (a total of 111) were inscribed in Greek: the 19 coins of Herod, the 7 of Archelaus, the 13 of Antipas, the 9 of Philip, the 9 of Agrippa I, and the 54 of Agrippa II (4 coins of Agrippa II, minted in 86 and 87 A.D., have Latin inscriptions alongside their Greek inscriptions). By contrast, the coins minted during those brief periods when there was Jewish political independence were inscribed in Hebrew: the 32 coins of the Maccabees (one has the Aramaic inscription, seven have Hebrew *and* Greek inscriptions), the 17 coins minted during the Great Revolt against Rome (66-70 A.D.), and the 51 coins minted by Bar-Cochba (132-135 A.D.).

University, are the most extensive ever undertaken in
Israel. Since the beginning of these excavations in 1968,
numerous inscriptions have been unearthed. It is signif-

Fig. 11. A fragment of the cornerstone from the uppermost course of
stones at the southwestern corner of the Temple Mount. The
fragment found on the pavement below among the rubble from
the destruction of the Second Temple bears the Hebrew
inscription which reads "To the Place of Trumpeting."
(Courtesy of the Israel Department of Antiquities)

icant that no Aramaic inscriptions from the Roman
period have yet been found. All the inscriptions that
have been found are either in Hebrew, Greek, or Latin.

Two of these inscriptions are worthy of note. The
first is an inscription on a large stone, part of the uppermost course of stones at the southwestern corner of the
Temple Mount. During the destruction of the Temple in
70 A.D. by Titus and the Roman Army, this stone was
pushed off from a height of approximately 115 feet to the
Herodian pavement below. There, Israeli archaeologists discovered it some 1900 years later. The
stone was broken in the fall and only a portion of the
inscription remains. It reads in Hebrew: *"leveit hate-*

ki'ah..." ("the place of the trumpeting...."). This was the spot where the shofar (ram's horn trumpet) was blown to announce the beginning and end of Sabbath (see Josephus, *Jewish War* IV, 582-583).

The second inscription contains only one Hebrew word—*corban*,* a word mentioned by Jesus in Mark 7:11, which reads:

> But you say, "If a man says to his father or mother, 'Whatever help you might have received from me is *corban*,' (that is, a gift) then he is no longer required to do anything for his father or mother."

The word *corban* is archaeologically documented for

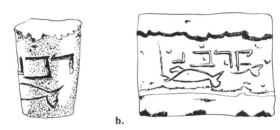

a.   b.

Fig. 12. a. A fragment from a stone vessel found in the excavations at the Temple Mount in Jerusalem bearing the Hebrew inscription *corban*, "sacrifice."
b. A wax impression of the corban inscription (a).

the first time in a non-literary context in this inscription.

At Masada, Herod's stronghold overlooking the Dead Sea, archaeologists excavated from 1963 to 1965 under the direction of Professor Yigael Yadin. The epigraphical evidence is staggering: fragments of 14 scrolls, over 4,000 coins, and more than 700 ostraka (inscribed pottery fragments) in Hebrew, Aramaic, Greek, and Latin. Here too, the ratio of Hebrew to

*Hebrew for "sacrifice" or "offering."

Fig. 13. **Model of Masada. The three-tiered Northern Palace of Herod and storerooms can be seen in the left foreground. The western siege ramp can be seen in the right foreground.**

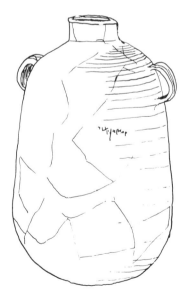

Fig. 14. **A storage jar from Masada, on which the name Shimeon ben Yoezer is inscribed in ink. The name is written in the semi-cursive Hebrew square script.**

Fig. 15. The fortress of Masada looking from east to west. The three-tiered Northern Palace of Herod can be seen along the right edge of the mountain.

Fig. 16. Aerial view of Masada looking from west to east.

Fig. 17. Close-up of the storerooms near the Northern Palace of Herod in which many inscribed pottery vessels were found. Note the unexcavated storeroom in the left foreground.

Fig. 18. Masada. The eastern casemate wall in which the Zealot defenders of Masada lived. The southern ritual immersion bath (mikve) can be seen in the right background.

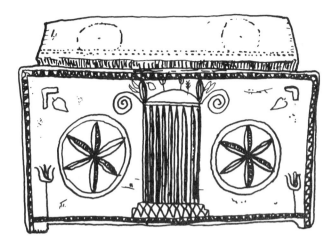

Fig. 19. A decorated ossuary from a two thousand-year-old tomb on
Mount Scopus in Jerusalem. The ossuary is decorated with a
fluted column with an Ionic capital in the center of the two
rosettes. A Hebrew inscription "kiria (or, "maria") shimon"
was incised on the side of the ossuary. The ossuary contained
the bones of a man about 40 years old and a boy about 15 years
old.

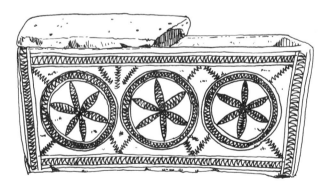

Fig. 20. A decorated limestone ossuary from a two thousand-year-old
Jewish cemetery near Jericho. The ossuary is decorated with
three incised rosettes and was painted red.

a.

b.

Fig. 21. a. Restoration of the position in which Jew from the first
century B.C. was crucified. This was determined from the
skeletal remains found in his tomb, discovered at Giv'at
Hamivtar in 1968.
b. The inscription from the ossuary in which was found the
bones of the crucified man. The inscription reads,
"Yehohanan ben Hazkul," i.e., John, the son of Hazkul.

a.

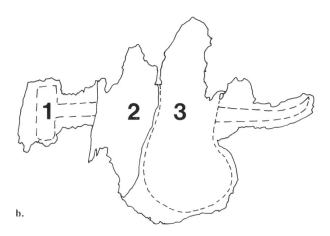

b.

Fig. 22. a. Drawing of the heelbone with board and nail piercing the
heel found in the ossuary above (see Fig. 21b.). The nail was
found still piercing his heelbones. A fragment of a board
that had been placed in front of the heel (see Fig. 21a.) was
still attached.
b. Cross-section of heelbone of crucified man. 1. Nail 2. Board
fragment 3. Heelbone.

Fig. 23. An ossuary found in a tomb-cave in the Kidron Valley in
Jerusalem (Length: 55 cm.; Width: 28 cm.; Height: 29 cm.)
along with about 20 other ossuaries, most bearing names,
apparently all of one family. The inscription reads *Imma*
("mommy") which, like*Abba* ("daddy," see page 32),was an
Aramaic loan word in common use among Hebrew speakers.
(Courtesy of the Israel Department of Antiquities)

Fig. 24. An ossuary found in a tomb-cave in the Valley of Rephaim in
Jerusalem. Length: 50 cm.; Width: 30 cm.; Height: 39 cm.
Three generations of the same family were buried in this tomb.
The Hebrew inscription reads: "The sons [i.e., family
members] of Eleazar" (Courtesy of the Israel Department of
Antiquities).

Aramaic exceeds nine to one.

Further epigraphic evidence can be found on ossuaries (stone burial containers). In Jewish burial in this
period the bones of the deceased were collected exactly

Fig. 25. The Hebrew name "Jesus" *(Yeshua)* as it was written on an
ossuary dating from the time of Jesus found in a rock-cut tomb
in the vicinity of Jerusalem.

one year after death and reinterred in a small container
carved from stone. These boxes were generally decorated with geometric or other designs, and often inscribed with the name of the deceased. Sometimes, the
bones of a man and wife were collected and placed in the
same ossuary.

These inscriptions were usually scratched on the ossuary by a family member or friend, rather than a skilled
craftsman. Thus, they are an important indication of the
spoken and written language of the common people, as
Milik has pointed out:

> The presence of Hebrew, besides Greek and
> Aramaic, on the ossuaries (which represent
> the use of the middle classes) surely attests
> that this was a natural language in that milieu
> and not merely a religious use of the classical
> Holy Tongue. For instance, the Bethphage

lid, the paylist of an undertaker's employees, is in Hebrew (Milik 1963: 131).

JOSEPHUS

Josephus was a Jewish historian of the first century A.D. He was the commander of the Jewish forces in Galilee. Realizing that all was lost, he defected to the Romans and became their official historian. His writings provide us with a great deal of reliable information on Jewish culture and events of the first centuries B.C.–A.D.

In his writings, Josephus often refers to the Hebrew language when dealing with the history of the first century. It appears obvious from these references that Hebrew was the spoken and written language of the first century; however, the same scholars who contend that the New Testament references to Hebrew mean Aramaic, have also contended that when Josephus refers to Hebrew he actually means Aramaic. Grintz strongly disagrees:

> An investigation into the writings of Josephus demonstrates beyond doubt that whenever Josephus mentions *glotta Ebraion* [Hebrew tongue], *Ebraion dialekton* [Hebrew dialect], etc., he always means "Hebrew" and no other language (Grintz 1960: 42).

Grintz supports his statement with many excellent examples from Josephus. Only two will be quoted here. The first is from Josephus' *Antiquities of the Jews*, I, 33:

> For which reason we also pass this day in re-

pose from toil and call it the Sabbath [*Sabbata*], a word which in the Hebrew language
[*Ebraion dialekton*] means "rest."

Grintz concludes:

Josephus derives, as had the Bible, the word
Sabbath from the Hebrew *SHBT*. In Aramaic
the verb *SHBT* does not exist. Aramaic
translators use instead *NCH* (transcriptions by
authors) (Grintz 1960:   42-43).

A second example is also found in the *Antiquities of
the Jews*, I, 34:

Now this man was called Adam which in Hebrew [*glotta Ebraion*] signifies "red."

Grintz summarizes:

Thus Josephus derives *adam* [man] from
adom, "red." In Aramaic "red" is expressed
by *sumka*; there is no root *ADM* in this language (transcriptions by authors) (Grintz
1960: 43).

Josephus does refer to Aramaic words, but what
should be emphasized is, "Josephus never said of any of
the words cited in their Aramaic form that they were
Hebrew" (Grintz 1960: 45).

RABBINIC LITERATURE

The largest and most significant body of written material from the time of Jesus is known as "Rabbinic Literature." Except for isolated words or sentences, it is
written entirely in Hebrew. The best known of this literature is the Mishnah. The Mishnah, or Oral Law, was
transmitted orally until it was finally committed to writ-

ing about 200 A.D. by Rabbi Judah Hanasi. (Today's standard Hebrew edition by Hanoch Albeck is printed in six volumes.) It contains rabbinic rulings, customs, traditions, pithy sayings, and homiletical material. The Mishnah is only one of six works of similar length known collectively as "Early Rabbinic Literature." They are all written in Hebrew.

It may come as a surprise to some, but most of the difficult passages or problems confronted in New Testament studies could be solved through a knowledge of Rabbinic Literature. Many of Jesus' sayings have their parallels in Rabbinic Literature:

> Do His will as if it were your will that He may do your will as if it were His will [compare Matthew 6:10; 7:21]. Conform your will to His will that He may conform the will of others to your will (Avoth 2:4) [Compare I Peter 5:6].

Note the similarity between the Golden Rule (Matthew 7:12) and the following:

> Rabbi Eliezer said, "Let the honor of your fellow man be as dear to you as your own"(Avoth 2:10).

Similar is the saying of Rabbi Yose:

> Let the possessions [mammon] of your fellow man be as dear to you as your own (Avoth 2:12).

The saying of Rabbi Tarphon reminds us of Jesus' saying in Luke 10:2 (parallel to Matthew 9:37-38):

> The day is short and the task is great, and the laborers are lazy; but the wages are high, and the master of the house is urgent (Avoth 2:15).

Many rabbinic sayings have no direct parallel in the New Testament but sound so similar that one might think they were from the New Testament:

Rabbi Jacob said, "This world is like an entry hall preceding the world to come. Prepare yourself in the entry hall that you may enter into the banqueting hall" (Avoth 4:16).

Any love that depends on some passing thing, when the thing disappears, the love vanishes too; but a love that does not depend on some passing thing will last forever. Which love was it that depended on some passing thing?—the love of Ammon and Tamar [II Samuel 13:1 ff.]. And which love was it that did not depend on some passing thing?—the love of David and Jonathan [II Samuel 1:26] (Avoth 5:16).

Judah the son of Tema said, "Be as strong as the leopard and as swift as the eagle, as fleet as the gazelle and as brave as the lion to do the will of your Father which is in heaven" (Avoth 5:20).

The Midrash

The Midrash (rabbinic commentary on Scripture), even Midrash written hundreds of years after the time of Jesus, is almost entirely Hebrew, and is only occasionally interspersed with Aramaic words, phrases, or sentences. The following is an example of homiletical material from the Midrash:

"As long as Moses held up his hands, Israel

prevailed, but whenever he lowered his hands, Amalek prevailed'' [Exodus 17:11]. But could the hands of Moses really change the outcome of the battle for better or for worse?—it is, rather, to teach you that as long as the Israelites directed their thoughts on high and kept their hearts in subjection to their Father in heaven, they prevailed; otherwise, they suffered defeat. You could say the same about the verse, ''Make yourself a fiery serpent and mount it upon a standard, and if anyone who is bitten looks at it, he shall recover'' [Numbers 21:8]. But could the serpent kill, or could the serpent heal?—it is, rather, to teach you that as long as the Israelites directed their thoughts on high and kept their hearts in subjection to their Father in heaven, they were healed; otherwise, they wasted away (Rosh Hashana 3:8).

Jewish Prayers

Jewish prayers, some of which date from the time of Jesus and before, are also almost entirely Hebrew. The following prayers are strongly reminiscent of the Lord's Prayer:

> May Your will be done in Heaven above,
> and grant peace and contentment to those who
>   fear You
> and do whatever seems best to You
> (Tosefta Berachoth 3:7)

May it be Your will,
O Lord, my God,
to make me familiar with Your Law,
and cause me to adhere to Your commandments.
Do not lead me into sin,
nor into iniquity,
nor into temptation,
nor into dishonor.
Compel my impulses to serve You,
and keep me far from an evil man
   or evil companions.
Give me good desires and good companions
   in this life.
And let me this day and every day find
   grace, favor and mercy in
   Your eyes and in the eyes
   of all who see me,
and grant me Your best blessings.
Blessed are You, O Lord,
who grants Your best blessings
   to Your people, Israel
(Berachoth 60b).

Rabbinic Parables

In the Gospels we see that one of Jesus' favorite methods of teaching is the parable. Rabbinic Literature contains almost 5,000 parables. Only two are known in Aramaic! The following is an example of a rabbinic parable:

He whose wisdom is greater than his works,
what is he like? A tree whose branches are

many but whose roots are few, and the wind comes and uproots it and overturns it. But he whose works are greater than his wisdom, what is he like? A tree whose branches are few but whose roots are many. Even if all the winds were to come against it, they could not move it (Avoth 3:18) [Note the close parallel with Matthew 7:24-27].

A special type of parable is the "king parable," a form often used by Jesus. The rabbinic "king parables" were collected by I. Ziegler and published in Breslau in 1903. Ziegler listed some 850 such king parables. Here is an example preceded by a typical dialogue between a rabbi and his disciples:

Rabbi Eliezer said, "Repent one day before your death." His disciples asked him, "But can a man know on what day he will die?" He said, "So much the more must he repent today. Perhaps he will die tomorrow. It follows that a man should repent every day. Thus in his wisdom Solomon said: 'Let your garments always be white, and let not oil be lacking on your head' " [Ecclesiastes 9:8].

Rabbi Johannan the son of Zacchaeus told a parable: "It is like a king who invited his servants to a feast and did not set a time for them to arrive. The wise adorned themselves and waited by the door of the palace, for they said, 'Is there anything lacking in a palace?' The follish continued working, for they said, 'Is a feast ever given without preparation?' Suddenly the king summoned his servants. The wise entered the palace adorned as they were, but the foolish entered in their working clothes. The king rejoiced when he saw the wise, but was angry when he saw the foolish, and said, 'Those who adorned themselves for the feast shall sit down and eat and drink; but those who did not adorn themselves for the feast shall stand and look on!'" (Shabbath 153a).

Note the striking similarity between the above parable and the Parable of the Ten Virgins in Matthew 25:1-13.

Here is another example of a "king parable" from Rabbinic Literature, followed by its interpretation:

The matter may be compared to a king who arranged a banquet and invited guests to it. The king issued a decree which stated, "Each guest must bring something on which to recline." Some brought carpets, others brought mattresses or pads or cushions or stools, while still others brought logs or stones. The king observed what they had done, and said, "Let each man sit on what he brought." Those who had to sit on wood or stone murmured against the king. They said, "Is it respectful for the king, that we, his guests, should be seated on wood and stone?" When the king heard this, he said to them, "It is not enough that you have disgraced with your wood and stone the palace which was erected for me at great cost, but you dare to invent a complaint against me! The lack of respect paid to you is the result of your own action."

Similarly, in the Hereafter, the wicked will be sentenced to Gehinnom and will murmur against the Holy One, Blessed be He, saying, "We sought His salvation. How could such a fate befall us?" He will answer them, "When you were on earth did you not quarrel and slander and do evil? Were you not responsible for strife and violence? That is why it is written, 'All you that kindle a fire, that encircle yourselves with firebrands, walk in the flame of your fire and among the brands that you have kindled' [Isaiah 50:11]. If you say, 'This we have from Your hand,' it is not so; you have brought it on yourselves, and therefore, 'you will lie down in torment'" [ibid] (Ecclesiastes Rabbah 3:9).

Note the similarities between this parable and the Parable of the Banquet in Matthew 22:1-14 (parallel to Luke 14:16-24). Also compare Matthew 7:21-23 and 25:41-46.

Jesus' Parables

Rabbinic parables give us a clear indication of the language in which Jesus taught. Jesus was thoroughly versed in the written and oral law. As we noted above, he followed rabbinic custom and taught in parables, often using "king parables." Like the other rabbis of the first century, he would certainly have communicated his parables in Hebrew.*

*The rabbis were the Bible teachers and preachers of their day. They taught the common people, often using parables to make their points clear. That they taught exclusively in Hebrew is highly significant. Can proponents of the Aramaic theory supply the name of even one first-century,

There is also textual evidence to prove that Jesus delivered his parables in Hebrew. Note how Hebraic they are, as illustrated by the Parable of the Prodigal Son:

> ...*and* his father saw him,*and* had compassion *and* ran,*and* fell on his neck, *and* kissed him...*And* the father said to his servants, "Bring quickly the best robe, *and* put it on him, *and* put [literally, "give," a Hebrew idiom] a ring on his hand and sandals on his feet, *and* bring the fattened calf, *and* kill it, *and* let us eat *and* make merry..." (Luke 15:20,22,23).

This passage is an excellent example of one of the characteristic features of Hebrew syntax. Greek, like other European languages, does not have this kind of sentence structure with the conjunction "and" appearing over and over again. Greek prefers to subordinate an independent clause to the main clause of the sentence. For example: "When I woke up, I got dressed. As soon as I ate breakfast, I brushed my teeth. After I read the morning newspaper, I drove to work." Hebrew, on the other hand, prefers to join clauses with the conjunction "and."* To the European, this continual use of "and" is distracting and sometimes irritating. In Hebrew, the above example would read: "*And* I woke up, *and* I

---

*Aramaic, like Hebrew and other Semitic languages, also regularly joins clauses with "and"; but Aramaic, particularly Biblical Aramaic, uses "and" noticeably less than Hebrew.

---

native-born, Palestinian rabbi who taught in Aramaic? (Hillel, it is true, is sometimes quoted in Aramaic, but Hillel was an immigrant from Babylon.)

got dressed, *and* I ate breakfast, *and* I brushed my teeth, *and* I read the morning newspaper, *and* I drove to work.''

We often see this same syntax in the Old Testament. The authors' very literal translation of a brief passage below will serve as an example:

And the earth was without form and empty. *And* darkness was on the face of the deep. *And* the Spirit of God moved on the face of the waters. *And* God said, ''Let there be light.'' *And* there was light. *And* God saw the light that it was good. *And* God divided between the light and the darkness. *And* God called the light Day. *And* He called the darkness Night. *And* there was evening, *and* there was morning—first day   (Genesis 1:2-5).

This, as well as other grammatical features in the Gospels, is actually independent confirmation that the life story of Jesus was originally written in Hebrew. Why is it when we see features like the excessive use of the conjunction ''and'' in the Gospels, we do not recognize that the Gospels are derived from a Hebrew source? The English speaker has grown so accustomed to this style through reading overly literal translations of the Old Testament that when it occurs in the New Testament, he fails to recognize it as Hebrew style. He should immediately recognize it for what it obviously is—proof that the Gospels are derived from a Hebrew original.

CHAPTER SIX

THE EVIDENCE OF THE
GOSPEL TEXTS THEMSELVES

One of the best indications of the Hebrew origin of the Synoptic Gospels is to be found within the texts of the Gospels themselves. The Hebraic undertext is revealed not only in sentence structure but in the many literalisms and idioms present, which are peculiar to the Hebrew language. An inability to recognize these Hebraisms has caused much difficulty in the interpretation and understanding of many of the sayings of Jesus.

Paradoxically, those passages which seem impossible to understand are not nearly as apt to be misinterpreted as the passages which we think we understand, when in fact, we do not. With the "impossible" sayings,* we just throw up our hands and say, "Well, maybe someday I will understand." They are so obscure we make no attempt to interpret them. However, many sayings of Jesus seem to make sense in English translation, but mean something entirely different than what

---

*For three examples of "impossible" sayings, see pages 20-21.

we think. For example:

> The kingdom of God is at hand [or literally, "near"] (Luke 10:9).*

> Whatsoever thou shalt bind (or loose) on earth shall be bound (or loosed) in heaven (Matthew 16:19).**

> Except your rightousness shall exceed the righteousness of the scribes and Pharisees, ye shall in no case enter into the kingdom of heaven (Matthew 5:20).†

> Think not that I am come to destroy the law, or the prophets; I am not come to destroy, but to fulfill. For verily, I say unto you, till heaven and earth pass, one jot or one tittle shall in no wise pass from the law till all be fulfilled (Matthew 5:17-18).††

The above sayings all seem to make sense. The problem is that many words in Hebrew have overtones that do not exist in English. A Hebrew word often has a much wider range of meaning than its English or Greek literal equivalent. Since our English Gospels are derived from a Hebrew original, many of the English words do not mean what they appear to mean. As would be expected with a translation from Hebrew, we see the wider range of Hebrew meaning in many of the words used, rather than the more limited range of English or Greek meaning. For instance, in Hebrew, "house" means not only "a dwelling," but "home," "household," "fam-

*See the discussion of this verse on pages 88-91.
**See pages 143-149 of the Appendix.
†See pages 150-152 of the Appendix.
††See pages 152-155 of the Appendix.

ily,"* "tribe," "dynasty," "a Rabbinic school" (i.e., the followers of a certain rabbi—for example, "the house of Hillel"), and "temple." It can also mean "receptacle," as well as "place of" or "spot." In addition, "house of" followed by another noun, is so idiomatic in Hebrew that there are over 200 different idioms which begin "house of..." In Hebrew, "son" can mean not only "a male offspring," but also "descendant," "citizen," "member," and even "disciple."**

There is another clue to the existence of a Hebrew undertext. Many times when we read the words of Jesus in English translations, the meaning is still expressed, but in very bad English—in ways that one will not find in normal English usage. We do not always notice this because we have met these Hebrew idioms so often in the Old Testament. For instance, in Luke 16:23 we read that a certain rich man "lifted up his eyes and saw." Now, this is a beautiful Hebrew expression, but it is not good Greek, and certainly not good English. In English we would simply say that the rich man "looked."

When we speak of Hebraisms or Hebrew idioms in our Greek or English text, what we are really speaking about are "literalisms"—overly literal translations of Hebrew idioms. How can one detect a literalism? We detect a literalism in the same way that we can tell if a person, who is speaking English, is thinking in another language. If, for instance, we hear a person say in English, "Throw the cow over the fence some hay," or "Go the hill down and turn the corner around," we know that

---

*For a Gospel passage where "house" is used in the sense of "family," see pages 167-169 of the Appendix.
**For a discussion of the expression "son of peace," see pages 167-168 of the Appendix.

the speaker is thinking in German. If someone says, "Help you me to find the ball," we know the speaker is thinking in Spanish. "I want somebody a book to give" indicates that the speaker is Dutch. "We will be happy to receive your faces at our son's birthday party," indicates that the speaker is thinking in Hebrew. We can recognize the speaker's native tongue because every language has its own unique idioms and sentence structures. Often only the person who is familiar with the language of the idiom will understand the idiom.

Rigidly literal translations of Hebrew idioms often give the reader the wrong impression. It brings to mind the story of the little boy who thought that God's right hand was completely useless and that He had to do everything with His left hand because he had always heard that Jesus was sitting *on* the right hand of God.

We are all familiar with many Hebrew idioms from the Old Testament. For example, "Noah found grace in the eyes of the LORD" (Genesis 6:8), which simply means God was fond of (or loved) Noah. The expression, "to know," meaning sexual relations, is found in Genesis 4:1: "And Adam *knew* Eve, his wife. And she conceived and bore Cain." This idiom is also found in Luke 1:34, where Mary says to the angel Gabriel, "How will this happen, since I have not *known* a man?"

The words of Jesus are full of Hebrew idioms. Some of these are humorous or even ridiculous in English, such as: "cast out your name as evil," "the fashion of his countenance was altered," "lay these sayings in your ears," or "he set his face to go. . ."*

*Respectively, Luke 6:22, 9:29, 9:44, and 9:51. For a discussion of each of these idioms, see pages 156-157, 158-159, 160-163, and 163-167 of the Appendix.

Often whole sentences, even whole passages, of our Gospels translate word for word right back into the original Hebrew. When Jesus gave his commission to the disciples he sent out, he said, "Whatever house you enter, first say, '*Shalom* be to this house.' And if a son of *shalom* is there, your *shalom* shall rest upon him; but if not, it shall return to you" (Luke 10:5-6).* In English, needless to say, you cannot say "*Shalom*" or "Peace" to a house, nor can "peace" rest upon or return to someone. In Hebrew, though, this all makes perfectly good sense.

In Luke 1:13 Zechariah is told by the messenger of God that he and his wife Elizabeth would have a son, and that they were to "call his name" John. This too is neither good English nor good Greek. In English we would simply say, "call him John," or better, "name him John." The same Hebrew words were spoken by the angel Gabriel to Mary: "You shall call his name Jesus" (Luke 1:31). "Call his name" is a good Hebrew idiom occurring frequently in the Old Testament, as in Isaiah 9:6, "and his name will be called 'wonderful'. . ."

The above examples illustrate how Hebrew idioms have entered our translations almost unnoticed. The unfortunate part of the story is that many of these Hebraisms often go unnoticed by our translators, including those of our most recent translations. All of this is in spite of the statement that often appears in the Forward to a new translation to the effect that it is based on the most recent Hebrew or Greek manuscripts.

In the Gospels, as we have said, words do not al-

*See pages 167-169 of the Appendix.

ways mean what they seem to mean. Here are a few
more examples:

God remembered Rachel...
she conceived and bore a son.

"Remember" sometimes means "to do a favor for
someone" or "to intervene on behalf of," as in Genesis
30:22-23, quoted above. Are we to assume that God
forgot Rachel and then suddenly remembered her? Certainly not!

In Genesis 40:14 Joseph requested the chief butler to
"remember" him when he was restored to his position
in Pharaoh's court. Yet the butler did not "remember"
Joseph, but "forgot" him as is stated in verse 23.
Should we assume that Joseph only desired the chief
butler to think of him from time to time once the chief
butler was reinstated? No, Joseph was requesting the
chief butler to intercede on his behalf to Pharaoh. In
Luke 23:42 the thief on the cross requested of Jesus,
"*remember* me when you come into your kingdom."
Jesus did not wait to grant the favor. His immediate response was, "Today you shall be with me in paradise."

Yet the chief butler did not
remember Joseph, but forgot him.

"Forget" is another word which does not always
mean what it seems to in English translation. It can
mean "not to intervene on behalf of," or "to abandon."
As in Genesis 40:23, noted above, the chief butler "forgot" Joseph, or simply did nothing for him. In I Samuel
1:11 Hannah petitioned the Lord not to "forget," or
abandon her, but to "remember" her; in other words, to
favor her with a son.

The baptism of John, where was it from
—from Heaven, or from men? (Matthew 21:25)

By the time of the Second Temple, Jews had developed an aversion to using the name of God for fear of violating the Third Commandment. They substituted evasive synonyms for "God" such as "the Name," (an abbreviation of "the Name of the Lord"),"the Place," "the Power," and "Heaven" (as in Matthew 21:25 quoted above). In the phrase "Kingdom of *Heaven*" this substitution is clearly seen. In Luke 15:18 the Prodigal Son says, "I have sinned against *Heaven*..." There also, "Heaven" is a clear substitute for "God."

...and there were added that day about 3,000 souls...

"Soul" can mean "person," as in Acts 2:41 above (compare Acts 2:43; 3:23). It can also sometimes mean "self" (Luke 12:19, "And I will say to my *soul, Soul*..."); or "life" (Luke 12:20, "Tonight your *soul* will be demanded...," and Matthew 16:26, "For what will it profit a man if he gains the whole world and loses his *soul*, or what would a man give in exchange for his *soul?*).

Wisdom is justified by all her children.

"Wisdom" always has a positive connotation in English, but in Hebrew it can connote shrewdness, craftiness, or even stupidity. In the context of Luke 7:35, quoted above, wisdom is used in a negative sense. John the Baptist, who was an ascetic, was accused by the religious leaders of having a demon. On the other hand, Jesus, who did not live the life of an ascetic, was accused by them of being a glutton and a drunkard, and of associating with tax-collectors and sinners. Jesus replied, *"Wisdom* is justified by all her children." He said simply and clearly in Hebrew idiom, "You can tell whether wisdom is real wisdom or stupidity by the consistency or inconsistency of its arguments. Since your arguments are so inconsistent, it is a clear indication of your stupidity."

> My righteousness is near,
> My salvation has gone forth...(Isaiah 51:5)

In Hebrew, there are many synonyms for "salvation." The word "salvation" itself is little used.* Other words express this concept more powerfully. "Righteousness" is one of the synonyms for "salvation." Zion is called "the city of *righteousness*" (Isaiah 1:10). The branch of David is called "The LORD is our *righteousness*" (Jeremiah 23:6, 33:16). In great distress, David asks God to pour out His wrath on his enemies: "Let them not come into Your *righteousness*. May they be blotted out of the book of life, and not be recorded with the righteous" (Psalms 69:27-28). Jesus. exhorts his disciples to "seek first His Kingdom and His *righteousness...*" (Matthew 6:33). Those who "hunger and thirst for *righteousness*" are blessed (Matthew 5:6). Of such people is the Kingdom of Heaven made up.

> Here is my servant whom I have chosen,
> my beloved in whom my soul delights.
> I will put my spirit on him,
> and he will proclaim judgment to the Gentiles.
> (Matthew 12:18; Isaiah 42:1)

Even the Hebrew word "judgment" (or "justice") can mean "salvation." In the same way, the verb

*Contrary to what one might expect, the word "salvation" appears only four times in the Gospels.

"judge" often means "save." When David is in trouble, he cries out, *"Judge* me, O God..." (Psalms 43:1). The judges of the Old Testament were saviors or deliverers of the people, and not judges in the modern sense of the word. God is called "the *Judge*" (Judges 11:27; Isaiah 33:22), or "the *Judge* of all the earth" (Genesis 18:25, Psalms 94:2). "Righteousness and *judgment*" are the foundation of His throne (Psalms 89:14). Rachel called the son that Bilhah bore her "Dan" ("he judged") because, she said, "God has *judged* me" (Genesis 30:6). Over and over, the Prophet Isaiah uses "judgment" as a synonym for "salvation": "Therefore *judgment* is far from us; and righteousness does not reach us...We look for *judgment*, but there is none; for salvation, but it is far from us...*Judgment* is turned back; and righteousness stands at a distance" (Isaiah 59:9, 11, 14).

Jesus promised his disciples that they would sit on twelve thrones judging the twelve tribes of Israel (Matthew 19:28, parallel to Luke 22:30). Are the disciples at some future time to sit as judges meting out punishment to members of the tribes of Israel? No, they are to be deliverers or saviors! Jesus is referring to Psalm 122. In this Psalm, the city of salvation—Jerusalem—is the city to which the tribes of Israel go up, and there thrones (note the plural) of judgment (i.e., "salvation") are set up.

Of course, "judgment" is not always a synonym for "salvation" in the Bible. It is often a synonym for "destruction" or "damnation." How then can the English reader distinguish between the two meanings? He cannot, unless he is aware that the text he is reading is a translation from Hebrew, and unless he knows that in Hebrew the word "judgment" has additional meanings which do not exist in English. Equipped with that knowledge, he can do what the Hebrew reader does —decide on the basis of the context which meaning of "judgment" is demanded.

> Moses said, "The LORD God will raise up for you a prophet like me from among your brothers. Listen to him, to everything he tells you. Every soul that does not listen to that prophet is to be cut off from the people." (Acts 3:22-23; Deuteronomy 18:15, 18, 19)

"Listen" sometimes mean "to obey," as in Luke 9:35, "This is my Son, My Chosen; *Listen* to him."

> The Kingdom of God has come near you.

In Hebrew, "to come near" means "to be at." If we try to understand Luke 10:9 and 11, quoted above, by reading the Greek word *engiken* (translated "has come near"), we are in trouble. *Engiken* means "about to appear" or "is almost here." However, if we translate it back into Hebrew, we get an entirely different meaning. The Hebrew equivalent of *engiken* is the verb *karav*, which means "to come up to and be with," or "to be where something or someone else is."

The Greek *engiken*, or the English "near," mean: "It's not yet here." The implication is that the Kingdom of God is futuristic, not yet here. The Hebrew *karav* means the exact opposite: "It's here! It has arrived!"

When King Ahaz was in Damascus and saw the altar there, he sent a model of it and the exact dimension to Uriah the priest in Jerusalem. Uriah built it and had it ready when the king returned. II Kings 16:12 records: "And when the king came from Damascus the king viewed the altar. Then the king drew near (*karav*) to the altar, and went up on it. . .'' In other words, the king went right up to the altar, and stood right next to or beside it. He was right there!

Another instance in which *karav* is used is found in Deuteronomy 22:13-14, which states: ''If any man takes a wife, and goes in to her, and then despises her, and brings false charges against her and maligns her, saying, 'I have taken this woman, and when I *came near (karav)* her, I did not find her a virgin,' then. . .'' Here, ''came near'' (*karav*) is used in the same way in which ''knew'' is used in the Bible—that is, ''to come near'' and ''to know'' are Hebrew idioms for sexual relations.

We are told in Genesis 20:4 that Abimelech ''had not *come near*'' Sarah. Although Abimelech had taken Abraham's wife to live with him (verse 2), he had not had sexual relations with her. In Isaiah 8:3 we are told that the Prophet Isaiah ''*came near* the prophetess (i.e., his wife), and she conceived and bore a son.'' Again we see this idiomatic usage of *karav*.

Karav does not imply that there necessarily has to be any distance at all between that which is coming near and that which is being approached. This is most important for the understanding of such passages as Luke 10:9, ''the Kingdom of God has *come near* you.'' We can see how the Greek or English leaves the wrong concept of Kingdom of God: futuristic. The Hebrew leaves the correct concept: present tense—NOW! The Kingdom of Heaven or Kingdom of God is always present tense, ''right now,'' according to Jesus' understanding and in rabbinic usage as well. It is unfortunate that the Church, because of a Greek and/or English consciousness, has confused the Kingdom of Heaven with Jesus' teachings on his Second Coming (what Jesus calls "the coming of the Son of Man").

The concept of "Kingdom" is perhaps the most important spiritual concept in the New Testament. In English or Greek, "kingdom" is never verbal. It is something static, something to do with territory. But, in Hebrew, "kingdom" is active, it is action. It is God ruling in the lives of men. Those who are ruled by God are the Kingdom of God.

"Kingdom" is also the demonstration of God's rule through miracles, signs, and wonders. Wherever the power of God is demonstrated, there is His "Kingdom." "Kingdom" as the demonstration of God's power is echoed every week in the Sabbath prayers in the synagogue: "Your sons saw Your Kingdom as You split the Red Sea before Moses." How can one *see* God's Kingdom? It is only possible when "kingdom" is correctly understood as something which is verbal and not static. We see God's Kingdom when we see Him in action. In the same way, people saw the Kingdom when they saw Jesus in action. This is what Jesus meant when he said: "...if it is by the finger of God that I cast out demons, then the Kingdom of God has come upon you" (Luke 11:20).

Jesus also used "kingdom" to refer to those who followed him, the members of his movement. His disciples were now to literally be the Kingdom of God by demonstrating his presence and power in their lives. Jesus' charge to those sent out by him was: "Whenever you enter a town and you are accepted...heal the sick of that town and then tell them, 'The Kingdom of God is here!'" (Luke 10:8-9). It is necessary to paraphrase the disciples' proclamation (just three words in Hebrew) in order to maintain its force in English: "You have seen God in action. Through us God is now ruling here. Satan has been defeated. The miracles you have just witnessed are proof of it." The disciples' words were verified by the miracles God performed.

From just the few Hebraisms discussed above, one can easily see the importance of reading the Gospels Hebraically. Only when we begin to put the Greek of the Gospels back into Hebrew will it be possible to fully understand the words of Jesus. One can only hope that there will soon be a new translation of the Gospels based on a Hebrew understanding of the text.

CHAPTER SEVEN

RECOVERING THE ORIGINAL HEBREW GOSPEL

Dr. Robert L. Lindsey, for many years head of the Baptist Convention in Israel, and resident of Jerusalem for over 40 years, is one of the foremost Christian scholars residing in Israel today. Dr. Lindsey and a number of younger associates, including David Bivin, are actively engaged in study and research of the New Testament texts. Their command of the biblical languages and the cultural environment in which they reside provides them with a competency that is unique in their field of study.

In his book, *A Hebrew Translation of the Gospel of Mark*, Dr. Lindsey tells of his attempt in the 1950's to translate the Greek text of the New Testament into a badly needed modern Hebrew version. In the Introduction he writes:

> It is also generally held that the author of the Markan Gospel must have derived much of his information from Aramaic oral sources, yet wrote his book in Greek. Rather to my surprise the preliminary study of the Greek

text of Mark turned up the conclusion that the Greek word order and idiom was more like Hebrew than literary Greek. This gave me the frightening feeling that I was as much in the process of "restoring" an original Hebrew work as in that of creating a new one (Lindsey 1973: 9).

Recent research by Lindsey has clarified the process of the preservation and transmission of our Gospel material. The process can be briefly described as follows:

STEP ONE: Within five years of the death and resurrection of Jesus, his words were recorded in Hebrew (tradition states by the apostle Matthew). It was a simple and straightforward Hebrew biography similar to the simple stories of Elijah and Elisha recorded in the Old Testament. It is estimated that this original Hebrew *Life of Jesus* was approximately 30-35 chapters in length.

STEP TWO: Almost immediately, there was a demand by the Greek-speaking churches outside the Land of Israel for a translation of this *Life of Jesus* into Greek. As the translators wanted to preserve the integrity of the text, the resulting translation was slavishly literal, as were most translations in those days; and since books translated from Hebrew into Greek are much longer in Greek, it was about 50-60 chapters in length.

STEP THREE: Within a few years, very probably at Antioch, the stories, and frequently elements within the stories, found in this Greek translation were separated from one another and then these fragments were rearranged topically, perhaps to facilitate memorization. (What remained were fragments that were often divorced from their original and more meaningful contexts.)

STEP FOUR: Shortly thereafter, a fluent Greek author using this topically arranged text, attempted to reconstruct its fragmented elements and stories in order to produce a gospel with some chronological order. In so doing, he created still another document (the fourth). This author, even before our Matthew, Mark, and Luke, was the first to struggle with a reconstruction of the original order of the story units (represented by Steps One and Two). In the process of reconstruction, he improved its (Step Three's) gramatically poor Greek, as well as shortening it considerably.

It was only these latter two Greek texts, the "topical" text (Step Three), and the "reconstructed" text (Step Four), that were the sources used by our writer Luke. Mark followed Luke's work and Matthew utilized Mark's. Mark and Matthew, as well as Luke, had access to the "topical" text (Step Three). However, the texts of Matthew, Mark, and Luke show they did not have access to the original Hebrew *Life of Jesus* (Step One), or to the first Greek translation of that *Life* (Step Two). The Hebrew "Life" was lost, like so many other

Jewish books of that period (for example, Ben Sira),* undoubtedly as a result of the exile and persecution that took place following the destruction of the Temple in 70 A.D.

There is every reason to believe, as early Church tradition states, that the apostle Matthew wrote the original Hebrew life story of Jesus; but he was not the author of our first canonical Gospel, the first book of the New Testament. The Gospel of Matthew itself does not give us any indication as to its authorship. Why then was our first Gospel called Matthew? Probably because of the early tradition that Matthew wrote a Hebrew Gospel.

The process of transmission of our Gospel stories can be illustrated graphically as follows (see page   ):

Note that Luke had access only to the latter two Greek documents (Steps Three and Four), while Mark and Matthew knew the second of these documents (Step Four) due solely to Luke. All tried to reconstruct as best they could the original *Life of Jesus.* Luke seems to indicate this in his prologue. Luke desired, he said, to present to Theophilus an "orderly" account. This ordering is to be noted in Matthew and Mark as well. Now we can understand why so many of the Gospel stories appear in a different chronological order from Gospel to Gospel. For example, Matthew places Jesus' teaching on anxiety (6:25-34) after Jesus' words about serving two masters, whereas Luke (12:22-31) places the teaching on anxiety after the parable of the rich fool, even though

*Ben Sira, one of the books of the Apocrypha, was known only in Greek until less than 90 years ago, when fragments of the Hebrew text of this book began to come to light. Today we have almost two-thirds of the book in the original Hebrew, the most recent discovery of Ben Sira fragments occurring in 1964 at the Masada excavations in the Judean Desert.

The Transmission of the Hebrew Life of Jesus

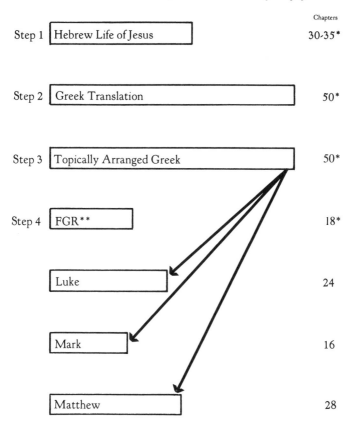

Chapters

Step 1 | Hebrew Life of Jesus | 30-35*

Step 2 | Greek Translation | 50*

Step 3 | Topically Arranged Greek | 50*

Step 4 | FGR** | 18*

Luke | 24

Mark | 16

Matthew | 28

* Estimated length of manuscript. (The blocks represent the length in chapters, and are drawn to scale.)

** First Greek Reconstruction

Fig. 26. The Transmission of the Hebrew Life of Jesus.

Luke also preserves Jesus' words about serving two masters (Luke 16:13).

Today scholars in Israel are once again attempting the type of reconstruction that was attempted by the writers of the Gospels of Matthew, Mark, and Luke. With all the current information now available this task of reconstruction is not only easier, but the finished work sometimes more accurate than that attempted 1950 years ago. Dr. Lindsey has graciously provided us with the reconstructed story given below (translation the authors'). Notice how much better we can understand the words of Jesus when Gospel story fragments are reconstructed to their original context.

In these longer contexts we can now see the actual teaching style or format of Jesus: he never seems to deliver formal sermons or addresses, but as he moves about the country with his disciples, he takes note of a situation or action, such as the woman putting her two small coins in the treasury (Luke 21:1-2). He affirms the action with *"amen"* or *"amen, amen,"* which in Hebrew is always a response, never a beginning (such as "verily" or "truly"), as has been understood by our English translators. He then begins to comment or teach about what has just happened, prefacing his remarks with, "I tell you...," and concluding with a pair of parables to illustrate the teaching.

THE MARY AND MARTHA STORY
RECONSTRUCTED

> ...he entered a village, and a woman named Martha welcomed him to her house. Her sister, Mary, seated herself at the Lord's feet to listen to his teach-

ing. But Martha was irked because of all the preparations that had to be made; and she went to him and said, "Lord, don't you care that my sister has left me to do all the work by myself? Tell her to help me."

"Martha, Martha," the Lord replied, "you are *worried* and disturbed about many things; only one thing is important. Mary has chosen what is better, and what she has chosen will not be taken away from her."

Then he said to his disciples, "Amen! I tell you, do not be *worried* about your life [literally, "*soul*"], what you will have to eat and drink; nor about your body, what you will have to wear. Isn't life [literally, "the *soul*"] more important than having enough to eat, or the body more important than having clothes to wear? Look at the birds, they don't sow or reap or *store* in *granaries*, and doesn't your heavenly Father feed them? Aren't you more valuable than they are? Can any of you add a single inch to your height by *worrying*?

"And why are you *worried* about clothing? Observe how the flowers grow: they don't toil or spin. I tell you, even Solomon, in all his splendor, was not dressed like one of these. If this is how God clothes grass of the field, which is here today, and tomorrow is used to stoke an oven, will He not more surely clothe you, O men of little faith?

"So don't be *worried*, asking, 'What are we going to eat or drink, or what are we going to wear?' (Don't be like the heathen) for the heathen chase after these things. Your heavenly Father knows that you need all these things. But desire above all else His Kingdom and His salvation,* and all these things will be yours as well.

"So do not be *worried* about tomorrow. Tomorrow will *worry* about itself. Each day has enough trouble of its own.

"The field of a certain rich man produced a good

---

*Literally, "righteousness," which in Hebrew is a synonym for "salvation" or "redemption." (See the discussion on page 86.)

crop. He thought to himself, 'What shall I do? I have no place to *store* my grain.

" 'This is what I will do,' he said, 'I will tear down my *granaries* and build bigger ones, and in them I will *store* all my grain and *goods*. Then I will say to myself [literally, "to my *soul*"]: "You have enough *goods* laid aside to last you for many years. Take life easy, eat, drink, and be merry." '

"But God said to him, 'You fool! Tonight you will die [literally, "your *soul* will be demanded"]. And then who will have what you have prepared for yourself?'

"There was once a rich man. He dressed in purple and fine linen and feasted sumptuously every day. A poor man named Lazar used to be placed at his gate. He was covered with sores. And as he lay there longing for a few scraps that fell from the rich man's table, the dogs would come and lick his open sores.

"Finally the poor man died and the angels carried him to Abraham's bosom. The rich man also died, and was buried. In Gehinnom* where he was in torment, he saw in the distance Abraham with Lazar in his bosom.

" 'Father Abraham,' he cried out, 'have mercy on me and send Lazar to dip the tip of his finger in water and cool my tongue, for I am in agony in this fire.'

"But Abraham said, 'My son, remember that in your lifetime you received your good things [literally, *"goods"*], while Lazar received bad things. So now he is here being comforted and you are in agony. And besides, between us a great chasm has been firmly fixed so that those who want to cross from here to you cannot, nor can anyone cross from there to us.'

" 'Then I beg you, Father,' he said, 'to send Lazar to my family because I have five brothers. Let him warn them so that they will not also come to this place of torment.'

"But Abraham said, 'They have Moses and the Prophets; let them listen to them.'

*Literally, "Hades," the abode of the dead.

> " 'No, Father Abraham,' he said, 'but if someone
> from the dead goes to them they will repent.'
> "He said to him, 'If they will not listen to Moses
> and the Prophets, they will not be persuaded even if
> someone comes back from the dead' '' (Luke 10:38-42;
> Matthew 6:25-34 = Luke 12:22-31; Luke 12:16-21;
> Luke 16:19-31).

As can be seen from the references, here placed together at the end of the narrative in order not to disturb its flow, we have before us four fragments of one complete story which is today scattered in four different chapters of our Gospels. Notice the key words (in italics) in these fragments. It is "worry," worry about the cares of life, that ties the first two fragments (the situation or incident in Luke 10:38-42 and the teaching in Matthew 6:25-34 = Luke 12:22-31) of this reconstruction together. The appearance of the theme "worry" in both fragments indicates they were originally united in the same context. The first parable clearly belongs with the second fragment because of the words "store" and "granaries." The word "soul" (appearing here in two of its Hebrew meanings, see page 85) also unites the second and the third fragments. And it is the word "goods" which helps to confirm that the above two parables are really twins and should be joined together. In addition, the theme of death stands out in both parables.

Of course, the main reason we know these two parables belong to this context is that together they illustrate the two principal concerns of life mentioned by Jesus in the second fragment (Matthew 6:25-34 = Luke 12:22-31). Jesus exhorted his disciples not to worry about the concerns of everyday life—food, and clothing. The two parables deal with these two themes. Both parables are about rich men whose only concern was for this world's goods. The first rich man had an abundance of grain (food), and the second was finely attired (clothing).*

Notice Jesus' very rabbinic use of doublets—two small doublets, "birds" and "flowers," in the main body of his teaching; and two parables to conclude and illustrate his teaching. To the Jewish audience of that day this was the most convincing method of teaching because Scripture says: "By the mouth [evidence] of *two* or three witnesses a thing will be established" (Matthew 18:16; Deuteronomy 19:15). As Joseph explains in his interpretation of Pharaoh's two dreams: "The dream of Pharaoh is one [a unity]...and the doubling of Pharaoh's dream means the thing is true..." (Genesis 41:25,32). Thus Gideon, to be certain God would really deliver Israel through him, laid out his fleece not once but twice (Judges 6:36-40).

And finally, notice how the longer context helps us to understand why Martha was so upset. We learn from the second fragment that it was not just Jesus that had

*In connection with the theme "worry" we cannot help but note two amazing rabbinic parallels:

"Rabbi Shimon the son of Eleazar says: 'Have you ever seen a wild animal or a bird practicing a trade? Yet they have their needs met [literally, "earn their living'] without worrying, and they have been created for no other purpose than to serve me. But I have been created to serve The Maker! Shouldn't I earn my living without worry?'" (Kiddushin 4:14)

"Rabbi Eliezer used to say: 'He who has something to eat today but says, "What shall I eat tomorrow?" is one of those lacking faith, as it is said, "enough each day for that day' [Exodus 16:4]. He who created the day, also created its livelihood.'" (Mekhilta de-Rabbi Shimon ben Yochai 16:4) [Compare "men of little faith" in Matthew 6:30].

arrived for dinner, but his whole band of disciples as well. Martha had a houseful of guests to cook for and she felt it was not fair of Mary to leave her with all the work.

Jesus taught that only "one thing" is important. What is it? Without the longer context we would not know what it is. But the second fragment (Matthew 6:33 = Luke 12:31) makes it clear that the "one thing" of the first fragment, the "one thing" of overriding importance, is to seek or desire above all else God's rule and salvation in our lives and in the lives of those around us.

If, until now, we considered Jesus a great teacher, when we hear his words in their longer context, we suddenly realize that the depth of Jesus' teaching is far beyond anything we had ever imagined. When restored to its longer context, the sophistication of his teaching is overwhelming. So vivid and alive is it when restored to its original wholeness that we are almost transported to that time and place. Suddenly, we are sitting next to Mary—at the feet of Jesus.

CHAPTER EIGHT

THEOLOGICAL ERROR
DUE TO MISTRANSLATION

The Gospels are rife with mistranslations. "But does it really make any difference?" the reader will ask. "Even if there are mistranslations here and there, does one really have any difficulty in understanding the words of Jesus? Are there any passages that have been misinterpreted to such an extent that they are potentially damaging to us spiritually?"

Unfortunately, the answer is yes. In fact, had the Church been provided with a proper Hebraic understanding of the words of Jesus, most theological controversies would never have arisen in the first place.

In the preceding chapters we have given examples of numerous mistranslations in the Gospels. Many, we have seen, go beyond simple mistranslation and adversely affect our theology. We noted, for instance (pages 88-91), that "The Kingdom of Heaven" is not futuristic, but rather a present reality wherever God is ruling. One easily gets the impression from the Greek text that although the Kingdom is near, it has not yet arrived. However, when one is able to put passages dealing with the Kingdom of Heaven back into Hebrew, it is immediately obvious that the Kingdom has already arrived, is in fact already here — almost the exact opposite of the Greek meaning.

The additional examples of mistranslation presented in the Appendix (beginning on page 119) will show, among other things, that a proper Hebraic understanding of the Gospels does away with the notion, suggested by more than one scholar, that Jesus never believed he was the Messiah and never openly declared himself to be the Messiah. We will see, for instance, that Jesus applied to himself the title "Green Tree." This was a rabbinic way of saying "I am the Messiah." It was a reference to an Old Testament passage which mentions "green tree," an expression interpreted by the rabbis in Jesus' day as a messianic title. Again and again Jesus claimed to be the Messiah by applying to himself such messianic titles as "Green Tree." He did not come right out and say, "I am the Messiah," because in Hebrew there are far more powerful ways of making that claim.

It is our hope to treat other mistranslations in a sequel to this book. Some of these appear to be important only as further proof that the original life story of Jesus was written in Hebrew. Others, however, have contributed to confusion, error, wrong behavior, and even spiritual bondage. In this chapter we discuss three more theological errors that are also due to mistranslations in the gospel text.

PACIFISM

It is widely accepted that Jesus taught a higher ethic

epitomized in his statement, "turn the other cheek." This has led to the belief that when attacked, one should not injure or kill in order to defend self, family, or country.

The idea that pacifism was a part of the teaching of Jesus was popularized in the writings of Tolstoy. Pacifism, however, is not today, nor was it ever, a part of Jewish belief. The Jewish position is summed up in the Talmudic dictum, "If someone comes to kill you, anticipate him and kill him first" (Sanhedrin 72a). In other words, it is permissible to kill in order to defend oneself.

Can it be, then, that Jesus was the first and only Jew to teach pacifism? It is very unlikely. We know that at least some of Jesus' disciples were armed (Luke 22:38; 22:50). Add to this the fact that at one point Jesus even suggested to his disciples that they purchase swords (Luke 22:35-37), and we begin to ask ourselves, "Did Jesus really believe or teach pacifism?" In reality, pacifism is a theological misunderstanding based on several mistranslations of the sayings of Jesus.

The first of these mistranslations is Matthew 5:21, where most English versions of the Bible read, "You shall not kill." This is a quotation of Exodus 20:13. The Hebrew word used there is "murder" *(ratzach)*, and not kill *(harag)*. In Hebrew there is a clear distinction between these two words. The first *(ratzach)* means premeditated murder, while the second *(harag)* encompasses everything from justifiable homicide, manslaughter and accidental killing, to taking the life of an enemy soldier in war. The commandment very precisely prohibits murder, but not the taking of a life in defense of oneself or others.

It is difficult to explain how English translators made this mistake since the Greek language also has separate words for "murder" and "kill," and it is the Greek word for "murder" (not "kill") that is used in Matthew 5:21. Even with no knowlege of Hebrew the English translators of the New Testament should here have correctly translated "murder," and not "kill."

A second saying of Jesus on which pacifism is based is Matthew 5:39[a], usually translated, "Do not resist evil," or "Do not resist one who is evil." Could Jesus possibly have said this to his disciples? If he did, his statement contradicts other scriptures such as, "Hate what is evil" (Romans 12:9), and "Resist the devil" (James 4:7).

Again, Hebrew provides the answer. When we translate this verse back into Hebrew, we see that Jesus was not creating a new saying, but quoting a well-known Old Testament proverb. This proverb appears, with slight variations, in Psalms 37:1,8, and Proverbs 24:19. In modern English we would translate this maxim: "Don't compete with evildoers." In other words, do not try to rival or vie with a neighbor who has wronged you.

Jesus is not teaching that one should lie down in the face of evil or submit to evil; rather, he is teaching that we should forego trying to "get back at," or take revenge on, a quarrelsome neighbor. As Proverbs 24:29 says: "Do not say, 'I will do to him as he has done to me. I will pay the man back for what he has done.'"

Jesus is expressing an important principle which

applies to our relationships with friends and neighbors. It does not apply when we are confronted with a murderer, rapist, or like person of violence; nor when we are facing the enemy on the field of battle. Jesus is not talking about how to deal with violence. He is talking about the fundamentals of brotherly relationships, about how to relate to our neighbor. If, for instance, a neighbor dumps a pail of garbage on our lawn, we are not to retaliate by dumping two pails on his lawn. If someone cuts in front of us in traffic, we are not to catch up and try to run him off the road. Wanting to "get even" is, of course, a natural response; however, it is not *our* responsibility to punish our neighbor for his action. That responsibility is God's. We are to respond to our neighbor in a way that will disarm and shame him for his actions. Proverbs 25:21 says: "If your enemy is hungry, give him bread to eat, and if he is thirsty, give him water to drink. In so doing, you heap red-hot coals on his head, and the Lord will reward you."

Once we discover how to correctly translate Matthew 5:39[a], we can then correctly understand the verses which follow. Each verse is an illustration of how we should react to a hostile neighbor. If, for example (Matthew 5:39[b]), a friend insults and embarrasses us by slapping us on the cheek, we are not to slap him back, but instead offer our other cheek. This, by the way, is probably the best-known of all the sayings of Jesus. It also is another of the sayings on which pacifism is based. Properly understood, however, it has nothing to do with battlefield situations, defending oneself against a murderer, or resisting evil. It is an illustration of how to deal with an angry neighbor, a personal "enemy."

Mistranslation of Matthew 5:39a has created a theological contradiction. But, when this saying is understood Hebraically, rather than contradict, it harmonizes beautifully with the rest of Scripture. Our response to evil *does* have to be resistance! It is morally wrong to tolerate evil. Our response to a ''hot-headed'' neighbor, on the other hand, must be entirely different. His anger will only be temporary if we respond in a biblical manner: ''See that none of you pays back evil with evil; instead, always try to do good to each other and to all people'' (I Thessalonians 5:15); ''Do not repay evil with evil or curses with curses; but with blessings. Bless in return — that is what you have been called to do — so that you may inherit a blessing'' (I Peter 3:9); ''Bless those who persecute you. Bless them. Do not curse them. Do not pay anyone back with evil for evil . . . if it is possible, as far as it depends on you, live peaceably with everyone. Beloved, do not take revenge, but leave that to the wrath of God ''(Romans 12:14, 17-19).

The responsibility of the godly person is to defuse a potentially divisive situation by ''turning away wrath.'' We are not to seek revenge. If a neighbor or friend has wronged us and is in need of punishment, God is the only one who can administer it properly: ''Do not say, 'I will repay the evil deed in kind.' Trust in the LORD. He will save you'' [i.e., ''He will take care of it''] (Proverbs 20:22). Our responsibility is not to react, not to respond in kind, to a belligerent neighbor. We are not to ''be overcome by evil,'' but to ''overcome evil with good'' (Romans 12:21).

GIVING WITHOUT DISCERNMENT

All of us are occasionally approached by someone with a request for financial or material aid. The request may come from a neighbor, a member of our immediate family, or even from a complete stranger. Usually, we grant the request. At other times, we do not. Whenever we turn down a request, however, no matter what our reasons may be, we invariably feel uncomfortable. The request may be unreasonable, or even impossible; still, we always feel a certain amount of self-condemnation for not granting it. After all, doesn't the Bible teach "give to every man that asks of you" (Matthew 5:42)?

It appears from this passage that one is duty-bound to give his material possessions to anyone who asks him for them. Is this really God's will? The Greek text of Matthew 5:42, and its English translation, force us to conclude that it is; consequently, whenever we fail to respond positively to a request for part, or even all, of our material goods, we are left with the feeling that we have acted in a way that is less than God's will for us.

A mistranslation in the first half of Matthew 5:42 is the cause of our confusion. This verse is usually translated:

> Give to him who asks of you,
> and do not refuse him who wishes
> to borrow from you.

This saying is couched in Hebrew poetry. One of the main characteristics of Hebrew poetry is parallelism — expressing the same thought twice, but each time in different words. Hebrew poetry is not rhyming the ends of the lines, but repeating or doubling the idea.* The second half of Matthew 5:42 repeats the thought of the first half. The verb "ask," therefore, of the first half of the verse should be parallel in meaning to the verb "borrow" in the second half of the verse.

Can "ask" ever mean "borrow" in Hebrew? Yes, the Hebrew "ask," unlike its Greek and English counterparts, has three meanings: 1) "ask a question;" 2) "make a request"; and 3) "borrow." In Hebrew, therefore, "ask" can sometimes be a synonym for "borrow."** Why are there two words for "borrow"? Because there is actually a subtle difference between the Hebrew word "ask" in the sense of "borrow," and the word "borrow" itself. In Hebrew, a distinction is made between borrowing an object, such as a book, which must itself be returned to the person from whom it was borrowed, and between borrowing something such as money or flour, which must be returned in kind. One is not actually returning the same flour, but the same amount. Speaking poetically in parallelism, Jesus uses the first word for "borrow" in the first half of the verse, and the second word in the second half.

Matthew 5:42 is actually one further illustration of Matthew 5:39a, "Do not try to 'get even' with a neighbor who has wronged you." Another way one might be apt to take revenge on a quarrelsome neighbor would be by refusing to extend to him a loan. Jesus states this in typical Hebrew poetical fashion. "Ask" in the first half of the verse is parallel to "borrow" in the second half of

---

*See the discussion of "parallelism" on pages 128-129 of the Appendix.
**For "ask" in the sense of "borrow," see Shabbath 23:1, Taanith 4:8, Baba Metzia 3:2, 8:1-3, et al.

the verse, and the meaning is the same. In beautiful Hebrew, Jesus says, "Give to him who asks you for a loan, and do not refuse him who wishes to borrow from you." Quite redundant in English, but elegant and powerful in Hebrew.

Once we put this verse back into Hebrew, it no longer provides any justification for giving without spiritual discernment and wisdom. This saying is not about giving at all; but again, about how one should react to a hostile neighbor. Certainly generosity is taught in the Bible, as well as helping the poor, needy, and elderly. However, we are not commanded to turn over our possessions to anyone who might ask for them.

We are admonished to be good stewards of what God has entrusted to us (Compare, for instance, the Parable of the Talents in Matthew 25:14-30). One is not to foolishly dispose of his possessions, nor to give without God's leading in the giving.

THE THEOLOGY OF MARTYRDOM

A mistranslation of the eighth beatitude may also have been the cause of erroneous theology. Matthew 5:10 reads: "Blessed are they which are persecuted for righteousness' sake, for theirs is the kingdom of heaven." On the basis of this translation, one would quite naturally assume that there is some religious merit in being persecuted for the sake of the Kingdom of God. Early in the second century A.D. this idea developed and found its fruition in the martyrdom of millions during the years of the ten severe persecutions until the Edict of Toleration by Constantine in 311 A.D. The idea of gaining religious merit through suffering persecution or through martyrdom has continued in the theological consciousness of the ecclesiastical church to the present day. Is this really what Jesus is referring to in Matthew 5:10? Does Jesus mean that religious merit can be obtained by suffering persecution? Are we to seek persecution? No! This eighth beatitude should be translated: "How blessed are those who pursue righteousness, for of these is the Kingdom of Heaven."

There are actually four mistranslations in this one verse. We should not translate "persecute," but "pursue." Secondly, "righteousness" is an unfortunate translation in English. "Salvation" or "redemption" would be more accurate (See our discussion on page 86). Thirdly, "theirs" also leaves the wrong impression. We do not possess the Kingdom. The correct translation would be "of these," or "of such as these" as in Luke 18:16, "Let the children come to me and do not prevent them, for *of such as these* is the Kingdom of God." Fourthly, the Kingdom of Heaven is not futuristic, as is so often understood (See our discussion on pages 88-91).

In the eighth beatitude Jesus is not discussing persecution at all. He is describing people whose chief desire is for God to redeem the world. The Beatitudes are a description of the kind of people who make up the Kingdom of Heaven. This beatitude, like the others, characterizes the "Kingdom Man," who wants above all else for God to rule in the life of every person. The eighth beatitude echoes the fourth beatitude which speaks of those who "hunger and thirst [i.e., "desire above all else"] for righteousness," in other words, for God to save the lost. It also echoes Matthew 6:33 where Jesus says that we are to "seek first [i.e., "desire above all else"] His righteousness" [i.e., "salvation"].

Saving the lost was Jesus' number-one priority. He said, "The Son of Man has come to seek and to save the lost" (Luke 19:10). In Matthew 5:10 Jesus is again emphasizing that the kind of people who make up the Kingdom of God are those who want more than anything else to see God save the lost, those who pray, "Thy Kingdom come" (an exhortation which means, "Rule God, over more and more individuals").

How could "pursue" be confused with "persecute"? If one knows Hebrew, he can easily understand how this happened. The Hebrew word *radaf* has two meanings: 1) "pursue" or "chase," and 2) "persecute." It would make no sense, for instance, to translate Isaiah 51:1 as, "Listen to me, you who *persecute (radaf)* righteousness . . ."The context forces us to translate, "you who *pursue* righteousness." This double meaning of *radaf* caused it to be mistranslated in Matthew 5:10.

However, if we say that Matthew 5:10 has nothing to do with persecution, then how are the next two verses, which *do* mention persecution, to be explained? — "Blessed are you when you are reproached and persecuted and slandered for my sake. Rejoice and be glad, for your reward is great in heaven. In the same way the prophets of old were persecuted" (Matthew 5:11-12). Is reward for persecution not promised here?

When we look closely at the text we notice a sudden shift in the pronoun (in verses 11 and 12) from third person ("they," "theirs") to second person ("you," "yours"). This is a clear indication that these verses were not originally a part of Jesus' Sermon on the

Mount, but a part of another context or story. They were probably placed after Matthew 5:10 by the editor of the topically-arranged Greek text* because of the word "persecution," which appeared in both passages. Actually, Matthew 5:11-12 does not deal with the same theme as Matthew 5:10 (Compare the parts of the Mary and Martha story, pages 98 ff., which today are separated from their original context.). These two verses were, no doubt, given in the context of Jesus' post-resurrection teaching to his disciples. During that 40-day period, Jesus prepared and trained his disciples for what lay ahead. Jesus knew that he would die a criminal's death, and that, as a result, his disciples would be treated with suspicion and contempt. He realized that they would face antagonism and ostracism.

In Matthew 5:11-12 Jesus does speak to his disciples about persecution; and he does promise a reward to those who suffer merely because they are his disciples. Yet even here, Jesus was not urging his disciples to go looking for persecution or martyrdom to gain a heavenly reward. He was speaking about what the attitude of the disciples should be when they were cursed and slandered by their fellow countrymen. They were not to be discouraged, but were rather to rejoice in the realization that their predecessors, the prophets, faced the same kind of persecution.

Let us repeat the question that was asked at the beginning of this chapter: "Are the many mistranslations we

---

*For a description of the "topical" text see pages 94-95.

find in the Gospels really all that important?'' We believe the answer is an emphatic YES. We are concerned
about all mistranslations or misunderstandings of the
Bible, regardless of how insignificant they might seem
to be. If the Bible is God's communication of Himself to
us, and we believe it is, then knowing what He has said
is of supreme importance. Every communication of God
is important, and we are not willing that any, no matter
how seemingly insignificant, should go misunderstood
if we have at our disposal the tools to understand. Today, happily, those tools are available to us. As a result
of the archaeological discoveries and the textual studies
of the past 35 years, we are now able to understand the
Bible, and especially the words of Jesus, as never before
in the last 1900 years. With these tools now available,
no effort should be spared in correcting every mistranslation and in clarifying every misinterpretation of
the inspired text.

APPENDIX
by David Bivin

The following scriptures were mentioned in this book as being examples of passages often misinterpreted due to a lack of understanding of Hebrew idiom. These scriptures were mentioned in passing without being discussed or explained. Here is a brief explanation of each, interpreted in its Hebrew context.

1. MATTHEW 5:3 (page 19)"Blessed are the poor in spirit, for theirs is the kingdom of heaven."

In the opening beatitude Jesus couples "poor in spirit" with "kingdom of heaven." "Poor in spirit" is an abbreviation of "poor and crippled in spirit" in Isaiah 66:2. The Kingdom of Heaven is what Jesus calls the body of his followers, his movement. In Hebrew, "kingdom" can mean "rule" or "those who are ruled," but it is never a territorial designation. "Heaven" is an evasive synonym for "God." "Theirs" is a classic mistranslation, still preserved in all modern English versions. The Greek word translated "theirs" should be translated "of such" or "of such as these." We cannot possess the Kingdom. It does not belong to us; rather, Jesus is describing in these beatitudes the kind of people who make up the Kingdom. It is the "poor in spirit," the spiritually "down and outers" who have no righteousness of their own; "the mourners," the brokenhearted who have reached the end of their strength and cry out to God in despair and hopelessness; "the meek," those who have thrown away their pride. It is people such as these who get into the Kingdom and find salvation.

———————— • ————————

2. LUKE 23:31 (page 21) "For if they do these things in a green tree, what shall be done in the dry?"

Here is an example of a verse which is unintelligible in the Greek in which it has been preserved, but which makes perfect sense when retranslated into Hebrew.

Jesus is referring to the "green tree" and the "dry tree" mentioned in Ezekiel's prophecy against Jerusalem and its temple (Ezekiel 20:45-21:7). Allegorically, "the green tree" is "the righteous," and "the dry tree" is "the wicked." A forest fire, which God starts, sweeps through the forest of the Negeb. The heat is so intense that even the green trees are burned up.

On his way to a cruel death, Jesus is not oblivious to the women who are wailing and weeping for him. What a terrible destruction would soon sweep down on Jerusalem, engulfing them and their children! Like Ezekiel, Jesus is heartbroken:

> Sigh therefore, son of man. Sigh before them with broken heart and bitter grief. And when they ask you, "Why are you sighing?" answer, "Because of the tidings which will come. Every heart will melt and every hand go limp; every spirit will faint and all knees turn to water. It is coming! It will come to pass!" (Ezekiel 21:6-7)

The women were weeping for Jesus. If they had only known what was coming, they would have been weeping for themselves. "Don't weep for me," Jesus says, "weep for yourselves. If they do this to me, what will they do to you?" In other words, if this is done to the "Green Tree" of Ezekiel 20:47 (i.e., to Jesus), what will happen to the "dry trees" (i.e., to the less than perfectly righteous)? The "dry trees" would face the same fate at the hands of the Romans, and worse.

The Greek text reads, literally, "if they do these things *in* a green tree." To "do in" (someone) is a Hebrew idiom which means to "do to" (someone), and it is this idiom that has confused our translators. Some translations, the Revised Standard Version, for instance, attempt to make sense out of this verse by translating: "For if they do this *when* the wood is green, what will happen *when* it is dry?" The same idiom appears in Matthew 17:12 referring to John the Baptist: "they *did to* [literally, *"in"*] him whatever they pleased." There, because the context is so clear, the idiom "do in" has not seemed to cause most translators any trouble. But in Luke 23:31 there exists one additional difficulty: in order to understand, and then translate correctly, the translator must also know something about rabbinic methods of scriptural interpretation. In a very rabbinic way, Jesus is hinting in Luke 23:31 at a passage of scripture in the Old Testament. Our translators are not aware of this, many even translating "green *wood*" instead of "green tree."

In 1901 William Wrede,* a German scholar, proposed what he called *"Das Messiasgeheimnis"* ("The Messianic Secret"), a theory still widely accepted. Wrede suggested that Mark's Gospel was to a large extent an apology. In order to explain why almost a generation after the death of Jesus the Jewish nation as a whole had still not accepted Jesus as Messiah, Mark inserted in his Gospel the notion that Jesus deliberately kept his messiahship a secret. Wrede personally did not believe the historical Jesus thought of himself as the Messiah, or ever claimed to be the Messiah. He believed that was an idea invented by the Church after Jesus' death.

Nothing could be farther from the truth! Had Wrede known more about rabbinic argumentation and methods of scriptural interpretation, he would never have erred so completely. The truth is that Jesus seems hardly ever to have spoken without somehow or in some way making a messianic claim. Jesus does not come right out and say, "I am the Messiah," as we moderns might expect; but in a very rabbinic way he hints at Old Testament scriptures which were understood to be references to the

*See Bibliography, page 172.

coming Messiah. In this passage, for instance, Jesus refers to himself as "the Green Tree" of Ezekiel 20:47—a clear messianic claim.

———————————— • ————————————

3. MATTHEW 11:12 (page 21)"'From the days of John the Baptist until now, the kingdom of heaven suffereth violence, and the violent take it by force.''

This saying is certainly difficult to understand. It is not just ordinary Christians who have been stumped by it. There seems to be no satisfactory explanation of this verse even in scholarly literature. Apparently, a great deal of violence is connected with the Kingdom of Heaven. However, that does not agree very well with the rest of the teaching of Jesus. Many and varied have been the attempts on the part of ministers and scholars alike to explain this passage.

The key to its understanding turns out to be an old rabbinic interpretation (*midrash*) of Micah 2:13 discovered by Professor Flusser. Micah 2:12-13 reads:

12 I will gather all of you, Jacob;
   I will collect the remnant of Israel.
   I will put them all together like sheep in a fold,
      like a flock inside its pen.
   It will be noisy and crowed with people.
13 The breach-maker (*poretz*) goes through before them.

Then they break out.
Passing through the gate,
    they leave by it.
Their king passes through before them,
    their LORD at their head.

These verses are full of rich imagery. It is the picture
of a shepherd penning up his sheep for the night. He
quickly builds a fold by throwing up a makeshift rock
fence against the side of a hill. The next morning, to let
the sheep out, he makes a hole or a breach in the fence by
tossing some of the stones aside. He steps through his
''gate'' with the sheep following close behind. They
have been penned up all night and can hardly wait to get
out of their cramped quarters. Of course they push and
shove, several trying to get through at once, literally
breaking through, further breaching the little gate in
their eagerness to get out and into the green pasture.
Finally they burst out into the open spaces, rushing
headlong after the shepherd.

In Micah 2:13 the ''breach-maker'' and the king are,
of course, the same person, but in the rabbinic interpretation discovered by Professor Flusser they are two different persons: the ''breach-maker'' is interpreted as
being Elijah, and ''their king'' as the Messiah, the
Branch of the Son of David.

Now we can begin to understand what Jesus is saying. He is not only hinting at Micah 2:13, but also at a
well-known rabbinic interpretation of it. ''The Kingdom of Heaven,'' he says, ''is breaking forth [not *suffering violence*''], and every person in it is breaking forth
[literally, ''those who are breaking out break out in it, or

by means of it," not *"the violent take it by force"*]"
(Compare Luke 16:16, the parallel to Matthew 11:12.).
Two tremendous things are now happening simultaneously: the Kingdom is bursting forth into the world
(like water from a broken dam), and individuals within
the Kingdom are finding liberty and freedom.

In Matthew 11:12, as in the *midrash*, Elijah, or John
the Baptist, is the Breach-Maker, the *Poretz*. He makes
the breach in the rock fence and goes through first. He
has opened the way. He is the Elijah of Malachi 3:1 and
4:5-6, who goes before the LORD to prepare His way.
As in the *midrash*, Jesus, the King, follows John. Jesus
is the LORD himself, who leads the sheep through the
gate. It is a powerful image.

Jesus is again teaching his disciples about the Kingdom of Heaven, his movement. It started when Jesus
began calling disciples, during John's active ministry,
"the days of John the Baptist." Since then, the Kingdom of Heaven has been "breaking out." Notice that
this is further proof that the Kingdom is not futuristic.
The Kingdom is something that has been in existence
since the time of John the Baptist.

The Kingdom is breaking out, and members of the
Kingdom are breaking out. In Micah and also in the
midrash, it is the LORD and his sheep who are breaking
out. Jesus alters that figure slightly so that it is the *Kingdom* and its sheep who are breaking out. Though Jesus
does not refer directly to his own role as the shepherd
leading the sheep out, no listener could possibly misun-
derstand Jesus' stunning assertion—I am the LORD.
Elijah had come and opened the way, and the LORD
himself was leading a noisy multitude out to freedom.

———————— • ————————

4. LUKE 12:49-50 (page 21) "I am come to send fire on the earth; and what will I, if it be already kindled? But I have a baptism to be baptized with; and how am I straitened till it be accomplished!"

John the Baptist prophesied that The Coming One would baptize with the Holy Spirit and with fire (Matthew 3:11). As we learn from the Book of Acts, Jesus did baptize his disciples with the Holy Spirit on the Day of Pentecost. At that same time did he also baptize them with fire? Many Christians have assumed the answer is yes, that the baptism of the Holy Spirit and the baptism of fire took place simultaneously. They take for granted that the "tongues like fire" mentioned in Acts 2:3 are a fulfillment of John's prophecy about a baptism of fire.

Were these "tongues like fire" on the Day of Pentecost that "baptism of fire" which John prophesied? It seems very unlikely. When Jesus himself later prophesies about the Day of Pentecost (Acts 1:5, 11:16), he says nothing about fire: "John baptized with water, but you will be baptized with the Holy Spirit." In this post-resurrection saying of Jesus, he instructs his disciples not to return to Galilee, but to remain in Jerusalem for a few more days until they are baptized in the Holy Spirit. Jesus, clearly referring to what would take place on the Day of Pentecost, makes no mention of fire or a baptism of fire. Those Galilean disciples who remained in Jerusalem until Pentecost waited for the promised

Holy Spirit, but not the baptism of fire.

What John meant in Matthew 3:11 by a baptism "with fire" or "in fire" he clarified in the very next verse through a beautiful allegory:

> His winnowing fork is in his hand.
> He will purge his threshing floor
> And gather his grain into his granary.
> But the chaff he will burn
> In a fire that never goes out.

For John, as for the Old Testament prophets, fire was a symbol of judgment. Isaiah often used this symbol:

> Here comes the LORD with fire—
> His chariots are like a whirlwind—
> To vent his anger with fury,
> His rebuke with flames of fire.
> For with fire will the LORD
> execute judgment. . . (Isaiah 66:15-16).

Fire is an awesome thing. It can destroy a home in a matter of minutes, or a huge forest in a few hours. The Old Testament usually speaks of fire as "eating" or "eating up" ("devouring" in King James English). Hebrews 12:29, quoting Deuteronomy 4:24, pronounces: "Our God is a devouring fire." Fire is a perfect symbol of destruction, and thus a figure of judgment.

Luke 12:49-50 remains a puzzle to the English reader for the same reason that so many other verses of our Gospels do. These verses are not English, nor Greek; but pure, undisguised Hebrew. In just two short verses we have a whole complex of Hebraisms.

> I have come to cast fire upon the earth,
> But how could I wish it [the earth] were

already burned up?
I have a baptism to baptize,
And how distressed I am till it is over!

First of all, we should note that these verses are a
beautiful example of Hebrew poetry. Hebrew poetry is
not like English poetry. It is not rhyming the ends of
verses of the poem. It is not a repetition of the same
sound, but a repetition or echoing of the same thought.
One says the same thing twice, but each time in a different way, in different though equivalent words. This feature of Hebrew poetry is called parallelism. Parallelism,
the placing of two synonymous phrases or sentences
side by side, is the essence of Hebrew poetry. We meet it
repeatedly in the Old Testament. For instance: ''We
have no portion in David, and we have no inheritance in
the son of Jesse'' (II Samuel 20:1). Both parts of this
verse express identical thoughts. ''The son of Jesse'' is
a synonym for ''David,'' and ''inheritance'' is equivalent to ''portion.'' Another example of parallelism in the
Old Testament: ''I will ransom them from the power of
Sheol. I will redeem them from death'' (Hosea 13:14).
''Ransom'' is a synonym for ''redeem,'' and ''Sheol'' is
parallel to death.''

In our passage, ''baptism'' is parallel to ''fire'';
''baptize'' is parallel to ''cast''; and ''how distressed I
am till it is over'' is the equivalent of ''how could I wish
it were already burned up.''

To the English speaker such doubling is disconcert-
ing. It appears entirely unnecessary. For him, it seems
quite superfluous to say the same thing twice. He could
easily omit either of the doublets, either side of the parallelism. But for the Hebrew speaker this repetition of

an idea is the most beautiful form of the language.

Further confusion arises in connection with the tense of the verb "come." Should we translate, "I *came* to cast fire upon the earth," or "I *have come* to cast fire upon the earth"?

Hebrew does not have a sophisticated tense system like English or Greek. In English we can distinguish between simple past (he wrote), present perfect (he has written), past perfect (he had written), past continuous (he was writing), and past perfect continuous action (he had been writing). In Hebrew there is only one form of the verb in the past. All five of the above past forms of the English verb "write" would be translated in Hebrew by the same word—*katav*.

Surprisingly, the Greek verb "come" (*elthon*) of verse 49 is in the aorist tense. The Greek aorist tense, like the simple past tense in English, conveys simple action in the past: for instance, "I *hit* the ball" (a one-time occurrence at some past time). To express continuous action in the past or present, the Greek language has other tenses. *Elthon*, therefore, can be translated in only one way—"I came." It has no other meaning in Greek; consequently, to be faithful to the Greek, we are obliged to understand that Jesus is saying he came once at some particular time in the past. However, that does not make sense. Jesus is not speaking to his disciples about the past. He is speaking about the present.

The context forces us to translate, "I have come." In spite of this some translators, like those of the Revised Standard Version, translate "I came." They do not suppose that the Greek text is a translation of a Hebrew original, thus they transfer into their English translations a Hebraism which had earlier crept into the Greek text. When, however, an English translator of the Gospels realizes that he is translating a translation, and that Greek translators in translating Hebrew texts to Greek traditionally used the Greek aorist tense to translate the Hebrew past tense, he no longer is bound to always translate *elthon* as "I came."

Over and over the RSV translators make this same mistake in translating Greek verbs; for example, in their translation of Luke 19:10:* "For the Son of Man [i.e., Jesus] *came* to seek and to save the lost." Here also the context forces us to translate "has come" rather than "came." It is clear Jesus *came*, but it is equally clear that when he spoke those words he was still there, still on earth. He *had come*.

This confusion of the tenses has come about because the Greek translator of the original Hebrew Gospel often used the Greek aorist tense to translate the Hebrew past tense, a standard practice since the days of the translators of the Septuagint** (circa 200 B.C.). The moment, however, one puts the Greek text back into Hebrew, the confusion is eliminated. As usual, one must be careful not to translate the Greek, but rather the Hebrew behind it.

More important than the correct tense of the verb "come," is how to define "come" in this context. When Jesus says "I have come," the English reader immediately pictures Jesus leaving his heavenly throne

---

*Another example of this type of mistranslation on the part of the RSV translators is found in Matthew 11:19 — "The Son of Man *came* eating and drinking" (instead of "the Son of Man *has come* eating and drinking").

**The Greek translation of the Old Testament.

and, as the Servant of the Lord, coming to earth. But "I have come" may often be a Hebrew idiom denoting intention or purpose. In Luke 12:49 Jesus almost certainly does not mean "I have come" in a literal sense. He is using "come" in its idiomatic sense: "I *intend* to cast fire upon the earth"; "My *purpose* [or better, "My *task*"] is to cast fire upon the earth."

Another Hebraism to which the English speaker would be insensitive, but which would definitely jar a Greek speaker: a verb of motion followed by an infinitive—in this case the verb "come" followed by the infinitive "to cast." This is perfectly good Hebrew syntax, yet altogether foreign to Greek. To our surprise, though the Gospels of Matthew, Mark, and Luke were written in Greek, we find scattered throughout these Gospels numerous examples of the construction *verb of motion plus infinitive*. "He stood up to read" in Luke 4:16 is another example (verb of motion, "stood up," plus infinitive, "to read"). A small point, perhaps, and one easily overlooked, but another strong indication that behind our Greek texts is a Hebrew original.

Still other Hebraisms are evident behind the Greek of the second part of verse 49: "but how could I wish it were already burned up." Literally, the Greek says, "and what I wish if already (it) has been set on fire."

In the first place, what is the "what" doing at the beginning of this clause? The King James Version, as usual, gives a very literal rendering: "*what* will [= wish] I." But "what I wish" makes no sense in English. The difficulty vanishes, however, once we learn that the Hebrew word "what" can mean not only "what," as in

Greek or English, but also "how."* "How" is certainly its meaning in this context. With that meaning, and only with that meaning, can "what" be parallel to the "how" found in verse 50.

Next, we have to ask whether Jesus in fact wished the fire of judgment were already burning, as all English translations indicate. The Revised Standard Version translates, "would that it were already kindled"; and the New International Version, along with most other modern versions, translates, "how I wish it were already kindled." Is it conceivable that Jesus longed for the judgment to begin? No! That would make a mockery of all Jesus sought to accomplish—the saving of men's lives. One might translate this clause as if it were a wish ("O that. . . ," "Would that. . .") were it not for the "if" which follows the words "how I wish." "If" changes the meaning to "how could I wish. . ." Jesus is not eager for the Day of Judgment. On the contrary, he would probably prefer to postpone it indefinitely. "How could I wish it," he says. He is not willing that any should perish.

Jesus, it is clear, recoils at the thought of fire or judgment. But is he thinking of its initiation (its being "kindled"), or of its termination (the final judgment)? The confusion arises due to a Hebrew word ("burn") with a different range of meaning than its Greek and English counterparts. The Hebrew verb "burn" can be

---

*An example of the Hebrew word "what" in the sense of "how" is found in the Passover *Haggadah,* the liturgy of the festive meal and home service on the first night of Passover. At a certain point in that service the youngest participant asks four questions. He prefaces the four questions with: "How [literally, "*what*"] is this night different than all other nights?" (Pesahim 10:4)

used in the sense "be on fire," as in English or Greek. It can also have a second meaning—"start burning" (break out in flames); and a third meaning—"burn up" (be consumed by flames). In Exodus 3:2, Moses comes across a bush "burning" (first meaning). In the next verse, Moses says to himself, "Why doesn't the bush burn up?" (same Hebrew word, but with the third meaning). It is this third meaning which we find in our passage. Once we put the Greek of this clause back into Hebrew, then we are free to translate not only "already burning," but also "already burned up." Does "burned up" make more sense than "burning"? Yes, because then we have a better parallel to "till it is over" which appears at the end of verse 50.

If "burned up" is the correct translation of the last Greek word in verse 49, then all our English versions are wrong! The subject of "burned up" cannot be "fire"; it has to be "earth." Fire burns, but it does not burn up. A log can burn up and fire can burn it up (cause it to burn up), but in English one does not speak of fire as burning up. Moses did not say to himself, "Why doesn't the *fire* burn up?" but "Why doesn't the *bush* burn up?" We are forced to conclude that "it," the subject of "burned up," refers back to "the earth," and not to "fire."

From what Jesus says in verse 49, one can be sure the final judgment had not taken place, the earth had not yet been destroyed with flames. One cannot infer, however, that the fire of judgment had not already begun to burn, that the earth was not already on fire. In fact, as we shall see, the earth *was* burning. Jesus had set the earth on fire.

Verse 50 begins, "A baptism I have to be baptized."

Fig. 27. Archaeological excavations in the Ophel at the Temple Mount. Note the monumental staircase and the area of the ritual immersion bath complex in the center of the picture, at the juncture of the third wall with the southern wall of the Temple Mount. The southeast corner of the Temple Mount, known as the "pinnacle" of the Temple, can be seen in the right center.

Fig. 28. Dr. Blizzard excavating in the area of the ritual immersion baths at the Temple Mount.

Fig. 29. a. A ritual immersion bath, or mikve, found adjacent to the
monumental staircase leading up to the Double Gate at the
Temple Mount. The eastern edge of the monumental
staircase may be seen above the pools.
  b. Another illustration of the ritual immersion bath uncovered
in the excavation at the Temple Mount. The ritual
immersion bath complex lay between the monumental
staircase leading to the Double and Triple Gates in the
southern wall.

Fig. 30. The ritual immersion bath in the southern wall at Masada.
1: the water conduit   2: the collecting pool
3: the immersion bath connected to No. 2 by a pipe
4: A small pool for washing hands and feet before
immersion in No. 3.

This is simply a mistranslation. The Hebrew word for "baptize" (*tovel*) can be either transitive or intransitive, depending on the context. Thus a Greek translator could translate this same Hebrew word as either "I baptize" (I immerse an article), or "I am baptized" (I immerse myself).* Once we put the Greek infinitive *baptisthenai* ("to be baptized") back into Hebrew, we then have the possibility of retranslating the Hebrew as "to baptize" (transitive).

*Baptism in Jewish practice was the submerging in water of an article such as a cooking vessel or utensil in order to cleanse it from certain kinds of ritual uncleanness; or, the submerging in water of oneself in order to become ritually clean. Immersing oneself was also one of the initiatory rites, along with circumcision and sacrifice, performed by proselytes. A man (or woman) performing this rite was not physically assisted by another person. He walked into the water alone and dipped himself. John the Baptist (literally, "the Baptizer") was not down in the water with those who were dipping in the Jordan River. He was called "the Baptizer" because by exhorting the people to repent he caused *them* to get into the water and immerse themselves. The earliest representation of baptism is found on a fresco in a second century A.D. catacomb near Rome. This wall painting portrays John the Baptist, standing on the bank of a river, extending a helping hand to Jesus who is coming out of the water and up the bank.

Does the text make more sense when we translate, "I have a baptism to baptize" (transitive)? The answer is yes. If we translate "to be baptized" (along with all English translations of the Bible), we then lack a parallel to "cast" in verse 49. In order to have a proper parallel, "baptism" cannot refer to something Jesus must undergo, but rather, parallel to "cast," something Jesus brings upon the earth and its inhabitants; not something that is to be done to him, but something he does to others. The baptism of which Jesus is speaking is not his impending death by crucifixion, but the fire which he had started. The translation "to be baptized" spoils the parallelism, the poetry, of these two verses; on the other hand, the translation "to baptize" removes a difficulty of exegesis. Furthermore, if the original of Luke 12:50 is "to baptize" (transitive), then Jesus is more likely referring to the same baptism of fire to which John the Baptist referred. John said (Matthew 3:11) that The Coming One would baptize the people with fire, but John never said anything at all about The Coming One himself undergoing a baptism of fire.*

Although we have not exhausted the evidence in this passage for the existence of a Hebrew original, we have perhaps discovered enough to now be able to approach the original meaning of these words of Jesus. "My task," Jesus said, "is to set the earth on fire. That I am doing. The earth is burning. I have already begun to sow the seeds of judgment, and one day there will be a final judgment. But I do not look forward to that Day of

---

*Note that this misunderstanding of the word "baptism" in Luke 12:50 has given rise to our English idiom, "a baptism of fire," a severe ordeal one undergoes.

Judgment, that final moment—the moment of my Return—when men will no longer have a chance to accept me as Lord. How could I wish for that! I am required to baptize the earth, to judge the world. That is the task I have been given by my Father. But in the meantime, until that judgment is complete, how difficult it is for me! How I agonize as some men decide to become my disciples, and others decide to reject my messianic claims.''

Up to this point, we have ignored one important fact. Luke 12:49-50 is really only an introduction to the next three verses. Verses 51-53 restate verses 49 and 50, explaining and amplifying them. Verses 51-53 should, therefore, indicate whether our interpretation of verses 49 and 50 is correct.

Jesus was a prophet. So often we forget his prophetic role. He acts like a prophet. His speech is the speech of a prophet. And like the Old Testament prophets, he frequently speaks in allegory. Unfortunately, when a prophet speaks in allegory, he is hard to understand. Fortunately, he usually repeats in less veiled language what he has just said in allegory. This creates a doublet, the feature so characteristic of the Hebrew mind. We might call it an additional type of parallelism. The prophet delivers his message once in allegory, and then a second time in more straightforward terms.

A good example of this phenomenon is Ezekiel 20:45-21:7. The prophet Ezekiel speaks first in allegory (20:45-49), and then restates in clearer language (21:1-5) what he has just said in allegory.* From the second

---

*Another example is the allegory of Ezekiel 17:3-10 and its restatement in 17:12-21.

passage we learn that the "green tree" and the "dry tree" of the allegory (20:47) refer to the righteous and the wicked, and that *Teman, Darom,* and *Negeb** (20:46) are Jerusalem, her sanctuaries, and the land of Israel.

In our Gospel passage, Jesus first speaks in allegory (Luke 12:49-50), and then repeats in more explanatory words (12:51-53). Notice the parallels between the allegory and its explanation. Both "I have come"** and "earth" appear in the allegory as well as in its explanation. We can also easily see that "give division" in the explanation is the parallel to "cast fire" in the allegory. It seems obvious that verses 51-53 are a clarification of what Jesus has said in allegory. Now the question is: Can we understand the clarification any better than the allegory?

Verses 51-53 do turn out to be easier to understand than the allegory of the two previous verses. Jesus is causing division. The Hebrew word which must have stood in the original text means disagreement, dissension, or dispute. Jesus was not going to bring peace and harmony, but division and dissension. Even members of the same family would disagree about Jesus. One would become a disciple; another would not. This is undoubtedly the same dissension that the righteous Simeon had prophesied in the Temple: "this child is destined to cause the downfall and rise of many in Israel, and to be a sign that many people will speak against [a cause of division]... and so the thoughts of many minds

*Three Hebrew words for "the south."
**Another Hebraism. In English one would say: "cause division."

will be revealed'' (Luke 2:34-35).

The ''sign spoken against'' of Simeon's prophecy is Jesus himself. Jesus, as he himself declared, was a sign to his generation just as Jonah was a sign to the people of Nineveh (Luke 11:30). The people of Nineveh were forced to make a decision about Jonah and what he was preaching. Their choice was to believe God, who spoke through the prophet, or face destruction. They had to accept God's sign or reject it. The people of the generation in which Jesus lived had to make a decision about Jesus, and like the people of Nineveh, had to either accept God's sign or reject it.

Simeon in his prophecy speaks of thoughts being revealed. This, like ''the sign spoken against,'' is a reference to the controversy that would surround Jesus. The messianic claims of Jesus cause division, even family disputes. Each person Jesus calls is forced to take a stand for or against Jesus. His thoughts are revealed. His stand is made public.

In this sense, the judgment of which Jesus spoke in Luke 12:49-50, that baptism of fire which John predicted, had already begun. It began the moment Jesus started calling men and women to join his movement, the Kingdom. The final judgment would take place at Jesus' second coming; but in the meantime, people were making decisions which would determine their eternal destiny.* If they did not believe him, did not repent, they would be condemned. Furthermore, the men of Nineveh, who *did* repent, would be their accusers at the

---

*Jesus had said of himself that he would be a sign to his own generation (Luke 11:30). It follows then, that judgment began in the generation in which Jesus lived.

Judgment (Luke 11:32).

So much was at stake — life or death, salvation or damnation. For this reason Jesus was distressed.* He hung on every decision. He rejoiced over every sinner who repented. His heart fell at every "righteous" person who thought he needed no repentance.

This passage, Luke 12:49-50, is extraordinary in still another way. It is a saying in which Jesus indirectly claims to be God himself. In the Old Testament it is always the LORD who comes with fire** or who kindles a fire of judgment. "I will send fire" or "I will set fire" are recurring phrases in the Old Testament, "I" referring to the LORD.When Jesus spoke in the first person of casting or sending fire, his listeners must have been shocked. Nor is this the only instance in which Jesus hints that he is the Lord Almighty. Jesus never hesitates to speak or act like God.

Jesus is also like God in his concern for the sinner. "The Son of Man," Jesus says, "has come to seek and to save the lost sheep" (Luke 19:10).† Like a good shepherd, Jesus knows and loves every sheep. He would not think of abandoning even one of them which had somehow wandered away from the flock. This concern for the lost is what explains Jesus' anxiety in Luke 12:49-50. Until the Day of Judgment he is under great emotional stress; and yet, in spite of this stress he does not at all long for that day because then it will no longer

*Since Jesus was so distressed, since he was at that moment experiencing pain and grief, it follows that the judgment was to him a present reality, something that had already begun.
**Compare Isaiah 66:15-16 quoted above, page 127.
† Here also Jesus is equating himself with God, for Luke 19:10 is a reference to Ezekiel 34, especially 34:12. There, it is the LORD himself who says so emphatically, "I, I myself... will seek and save my sheep."

be possible to rescue the lost.

In the Second Epistle of Peter there is a striking parallel to Luke 12:49-50. Like Luke 12:49-50 it speaks of judgment, but also of the compassion and patience of the Lord. It is such a fascinating parallel that I quote it in concluding:

> God has commanded that the earth and the heavens be stored away for a great bonfire at the judgment day, when all ungodly men will perish. But don't forget this, dear friends, that a day or a thousand years from now is like tomorrow to the Lord. He isn't really being slow about his promised return, even though it sometimes seems that way. But he is waiting, for the good reason that he is not willing that any should perish, and he is giving more time for sinners to repent.* The day of the Lord is surely coming, as unexpectedly as a thief, and then the heavens will pass away with a terrible noise and the heavenly bodies will disappear in fire, and the earth and everything on it will be burned up (II Peter 3:7-10, Living Bible).

---

*Notice that both here and in the passage where Jesus speaks of the "sign of Jonah" (Luke 11:29-32), repentance is mentioned as necessary in order to escape the judgment.

————————————— • —————————————

5. MATTHEW 16:19 (page 80) "Whatsoever thou shalt bind (or loose) on earth shall be bound (or loosed) in heaven."

Due principally to the influence of the Septuagint, the second century B.C. Greek translation of the Old Testament, most Hebrew words came to have a fixed or standard translation in Greek. *Dein* and *luein,* for instance, the Greek verbs used in Matthew 16:19, are the standard translations in the Septuagint for "bind" and "loose." The Greek translation of a Hebrew word could normally be the equivalent of only one of its meanings, usually the first or original meaning. However, because the standard translation became so fixed in the minds of Greek translators, they employed it even when the Hebrew word it translated appeared in an entirely different context and with an obviously different meaning. In those days translating was an extremely mechanical and literal affair.

Such a method of translating is really a blessing in disguise for anyone trying to recover a Hebrew text, such as the *Life of Jesus,* which has survived only in Greek translation. It makes it relatively easy to put the Greek back into Hebrew. But this type of translating is anything but a blessing for the unfortunate English speaker reading an English version of one of these surviving Greek texts translated by a scholar who is not seeking Hebrew equivalents, and who mechanically translates the Greek into English irregardless of what the context dictates. When this scholar translates a Greek passage back of which is idiomatic Hebrew, he either translates literally, ending up with something which makes no sense in English; or worse — he risks an "educated" guess, ending up with something which is good English, but which has nothing to do with the original meaning of the Hebrew.

A case in point is the way English translators of the New Testament have handled "good eye" in Matthew 6:22. "If your eye is good" is an idiomatic way of saying in Hebrew, "if you are generous." But our English translators have not recognized this Hebrew idiom. Almost all translations preserve the singular, "eye," even though "eyes" would make more sense in English. Is it necessary for only one of the eyes to be good? Which one, the right or the left? Only three translations (Good News for Modern Man, New English Bible, New International Version) have felt the absurdity of "eye." These translations have translated "eyes" in spite of the fact that the original Greek text has "eye."

More variety exists in the translation of the word "good." Weymouth and the New International Version translate literally. But obviously, "good" in relation to an eye means nothing in particular. (Weymouth tries to solve this problem by translating "eye" as "eyesight" — "if your *eyesight* is good"!) Other translators simply guess at the meaning of "good." "Single" is the traditional translation of "good" (King James, American Standard). Most modern versions prefer "sound" (Amplified, Goodspeed, Jerusalem Bible, New Berkeley, New English Bible, Phillips, Revised Standard, Williams). Other suggestions are "clear" (Good News for Modern Man, New American Standard), and "pure" (Living Bible). Only James Moffatt translates "good eye" as "generous," but even he uses "sound" in the Lukan parallel to Matthew 6:22. (The same Greek word for "good" appears in both places.) Apparently, by the time Moffatt reached Luke 11:34 he was already beginning to have some doubts about his translation of Matthew 6:22.

The Hebrew words for "bind" and "loose" each appear with more than one meaning in the Old Testament. "Bind," for instance, can mean "tie up" (Judges 15:12, 16:11), "imprison" (II Kings 17:4), "hitch" a cart, wagon, chariot (Genesis 46:29), or "tether" an animal (Genesis 49:11); and by the time of Jesus the word "bind" had acquired an additional meaning — "bind" in the sense of "forbid." Similarly, "loose" had acquired the opposite meaning — "permit." These last meanings of "bind" and "loose" are the ones we most often meet in Rabbinic Literature. The Rabbis were constantly called upon by their community to interpret scriptural commands. Was such-and-such an action permitted? Was such-and-such a thing or person ritually clean? The Bible, for example, forbids working on Saturday. But it does not define "work." As a result, the Rabbis were called upon to declare what an individual was and was not permitted to do on the Sabbath. They "bound" (prohibited) certain activities, and "loosed" (allowed) other activities.

Interestingly, the Rabbis defined work as any activity involving the production, creation, or transformation of an object. Work, therefore, is not necessarily an activity which causes physical or mental fatigue. Study is allowed on the Sabbath. "One may spend the entire Sabbath opening and closing books until one drops with exhaustion and yet not violate the Sabbath. On the other hand, the mere striking of a match, just once, is a desecration of the Sabbath because it involves creation" (Chill 1974: 37).

The Mishnah is filled with rabbinic rulings on what was "loosed" (permitted) or "bound" (forbidden):

> During the war of Vespasian [66-70 A.D.], they (the Rabbis) forbade the garlands of the bridegrooms and the (playing of) bells. During the war of Quietus [116-117 A.D.], they forbade the garlands of the brides and that a man should teach his son Greek. In the last war [the Bar-Cochba Revolt, 132-135 A.D.], they forbade the bride to ride in a litter within her village. But our Rabbis permitted [literally, "loosed"] the bride to ride in a litter within her village (Sotah 9:14).

> If a man made a vow to abstain from milk, he is permitted [literally, "loosed"] whey. Rabbi Yoseh forbids it . . . If a man made a vow to abstain from meat, he is permitted broth [i.e., the water in which the meat was cooked] . . . Rabbi Judah forbids it . . . If a man made a vow to abstain from wine, he is permitted a cooked dish which has the taste of wine . . . (Nedarim 6:5-7).

He [Rabban Gamaliel] bathed on the first night after his wife died. His disciples said to him, "Didn't you teach us that a mourner is forbidden [literally, "bound"] to bathe?" He said to them, "I am not like the others. I am not well" (Berachoth 2:6).

If a man sold produce in Syria and said, "It is from the Land of Israel," tithes must be paid from it. If he said, "It is already tithed," he may be believed, since the mouth that forbade [literally, "bound"] is the mouth that permitted [literally, "loosed"]* (Demai 6:11).

The Greek translator of Matthew 16:19 has used *dein* and *luein,* the standard Greek translations of the Hebrew words "bind" and "loose," even though it is obvious that in this context these words mean "forbid" and "permit," and not "bind" and "loose." Jesus is giving Peter the authority to make decisions regulating the life of the Church. He confers upon Peter symbols of authority, the keys of the Kingdom of Heaven. Decisions or rulings Peter makes will have the authority of Heaven behind them. His decisions will be upheld by God. ("Heaven" is an evasive synonym for "God.") What Peter forbade, Heaven would forbid. What Peter permitted, Heaven would permit.

The movement Jesus created (the Church) was a

---

*In other words, the mouth that now allows this produce to be eaten, by saying it has already been tithed, this mouth is to be trusted since it is the same mouth that earlier forbade it from being eaten until the tithe was paid, by saying it was produced in the Land of Israel.

new phenomenon in Jewish history. Situations would soon arise which none of the Jews in this movement had ever had to face, situations about which the Bible gave no instructions, situations with which even the Rabbis, contemporaries of Jesus, had not had to deal. Decisions would have to be made, solutions found. Even more frightening, Jesus, their Rabbi, would no longer be there to make the decisions, to say what was permitted and what was forbidden. Peter and the other leaders of the Church would now take his place. They were not, however, to be indecisive for fear they would make wrong decisions. They had the authority to make decisions. God would be with them. He would endorse their decisions.

The Apostles, like the Rabbis, were called upon by their community, the Church, to interpret Scripture, settle disputes, and find answers in times of crisis. Sometimes they were compelled to deal with petty complaints: the complaints, for instance, of the Greek-speaking Jews that their widows were not being treated as well as the Hebrew-speaking widows in the daily distribution of food (Acts 6:1-6). At other times, the Apostles were required to settle raging controversies, controversies which had the potential of causing irreparable division in the Church. One such controversy is described in Acts 15 — the controversy over whether to admit Gentiles into the Church without first circumcising them and without commanding them to keep the Law of Moses. The decision that was reached is a classic example of how the leaders of the Church exercised their authority to ''bind'' and ''loose.''

The Apostles and elders convened in Jerusalem to

discuss the problem. There was much debate! Peter spoke (Acts 15:7-11), and then James (Acts 15:13-21). Peter's attitude was probably crucial, since it was to him that Jesus originally gave the authority to make decisions affecting the Church. Peter "loosed." He ruled that the yoke of the commandments was too heavy for former Gentiles (verse 10). These disciples should not be required to keep the Law of Moses. Peter released them from that obligation. James concurred. He too "loosed": "It is my judgment that we should not cause difficulties for those Gentiles who turn to God" (verse 19). But James "bound" (verse 20) as well as "loosed." He ruled that it was necessary for Gentiles who became believers to distance themselves from idolatry and cult prostitutes,* and to abstain from eating meat from which the blood has not been removed** (such as the meat of animals that have been strangled rather than bled to death). James forbade or prohibited three things.

Following their speeches, the rulings of Peter and James, including the prohibitions of James, were confirmed by the rest of the leadership, and later by the entire Church (verse 22).

---

*"Unchastity" is a poor translation. The Hebrew equivalent of the Greek noun always has to do with prostitution.
**The commandment not to eat blood is found in Leviticus 7:26.

———————————— • ————————————

6. MATTHEW 5:20 (page 80) "Except your righteousness shall exceed the righteousness of the scribes and Pharisees, ye shall in no case enter into the kingdom of heaven."

The scribes and Pharisees were extremely scrupulous in their religious observance. Are we to be more righteous than they if we want to "get to Heaven"? At first glance that is what Jesus seems to be saying, and this is how many of the best Bible commentators have understood these words. For instance, W. C. Allen, editor of the volume on Matthew in the *International Critical Commentary* series, writes: "For your 'righteousness' is to be not less, but more exacting than that of the scribes and Pharisees" (*ICC, Matthew,* page 46). However, almost every Christian instinctively feels the impossibility of such an interpretation. It just does not correspond to the teaching of the rest of the New Testament. How, then, are we to understand this saying of Jesus? The key is a correct understanding of the word "righteousness," and of the phrase "kingdom of heaven."

By the time of Jesus, the rich Old Testament word *tsedakah* ("righteousness" in the sense of "deliverance" or "salvation"*) had come to have a second, more restricted meaning — "almsgiving" (monetary help to the poor). In the eyes of the Pharisees, almsgiving, prayer, and fasting were the three most important

---

*See the discussion of the word "righteousness" on page 86.

components of righteous living. Almsgiving was the most important of the three, and so synonymous with righteousness that in time it came itself to be called "righteousness." In Matthew 5:20 Jesus is playing on these two meanings of the word *tsedakah* — the older, broader meaning ("salvation"), and the newer, narrower meaning ("almsgiving").*

In Jesus' day almsgiving had become a meritorious deed in some circles. Many Jews, like many Christians today, believed they could work out their own righteousness instead of submitting to the righteousness of God (Romans 10:3). But Jesus says: "If your *tsedakah* is not bigger than the *tsedakah* of the scribes and Pharisees — in other words, if it is the undersized *tsedakah* of the scribes and Pharisees, and not that mighty *tsedakah* of which the prophets spoke — then you are not going to get into the Kingdom of Heaven."

And what is the Kingdom of Heaven? We must remember that the Kingdom of Heaven is not futuristic.** "Kingdom of Heaven" is Jesus' name for his movement, the body of his disciples; and "to enter or come into the Kingdom of Heaven" means to become a disciple or believer. (It does not mean "to go to heaven.)

If your righteousness or salvation is reduced to almsgiving, Jesus admonishes, you are not going to be in my movement, the Kingdom of Heaven. If it is your

*Matthew 5:20 fits naturally after Matthew 6:1. That must have been its location in the original Hebrew Gospel. Matthew 6:1, like Matthew 5:20, is a warning. It is also a heading for the three illustrations which immediately follow: on almsgiving (Matthew 6:2-4; on prayer (Matthew 6:5-8; on fasting (Matthew 6:16-18). Not surprisingly, Matthew 6:1 begins: "Be careful not to *do your righteousness* publicly." Note that the word "hypocrites" appears in all three illusrations.

** See pages 88-91 and 125.

tsedakah, and not God's *tsedakah,* you are going to miss God's *tsedakah* (salvation) altogether. You will not find it because you will be looking for it in the wrong place.

————————————— • —————————————

7. MATTHEW 5:17-18 (page 80) "Think not that I am come to destroy the law, or the prophets; I am not come to destroy, but to fulfill. For verily, I say unto you, till heaven and earth pass, one jot or one tittle shall in no wise pass from the law till all be fulfilled."

In Matthew 5:17, Jesus claims he has no intention of abolishing or suspending the Mosaic Law. For most Christians, this comes as a shock. After all, did not the Apostle Paul say, "Christ is the end of the Law" (Romans 10:4)?* Jesus' statement seems such a contradiction that many Christian commentators have tried to explain it away by suggesting that his words do not really mean what they seem to mean. Their attempts are futile. The meaning of Jesus' words is clear. As long as the world lasts, he goes on to say in verse 18, the Law will last. Here Jesus is in complete agreement with the Rabbis: "Everything has an end** — heaven and earth

---

*Here Paul is not using "Law" *(Torah)* in its original sense, but in its later rabbinic sense. Originally, the word *torah* meant "instruction." Later it also came to mean, in rabbinic usage, the sum total of the commandments, both oral and written, by which a man, through adherence to them, could be counted righteous in God's sight.
**Or "limit."

have an end — except one thing which has no end. And what is that? The Law" (Genesis Rabbah 10:1); "... no letter shall ever be abolished from the Law" (Exodus Rabbah 6:1); "Should all the nations of the world unite to uproot one word of the Law, they would be unable to do it" (Leviticus Rabbah 19:2).

Other commentators have emphasized the word "fulfill" in verse 17. According to their interpretation, something was lacking in the Law. Jesus completed or fulfilled the Law. He did not do away with the Law. He simply filled up what was lacking. And what was it that was lacking in the law? The Messiah. Jesus fulfilled the Law, that is, he fulfilled the messianic prophecies found in the Law (and the Prophets). In other words, in Jesus, the Law reached its zenith. Rather than being destroyed, it now existed as God originally intended. It had come to an end in one form, but continued in another, more perfect form.

This interpretation also has its problems. True, Jesus *is* the fulfillment of the Law, and only in acceptance of him as Messiah is there now salvation; but is that the point Jesus is making in verse 17? If he is saying he is "the end of the Law," then why does he say in the next verse that the Law will never disappear? If, in verse 17, Jesus is stressing the messianic fulfillment of the Law, then verse 17 is in conflict with verse 18.

There is something exasperating about trying to understand a verse like this. The meaning is apparently locked up. What the verse seems to say contradicts what we know from other verses in the New Testament. The truth is that we cannot be expected to understand this verse. Like so many other verses in our English Gospels it is incomprehensible. Nor are we any better off with the "original" Greek of this verse. The Greek is just as impenetrable. As usual, the only solution is to put the Greek back into Hebrew. Once we set this passage in its Hebrew context it makes sense.

It is unnecessary to repeat all of what was said above (pages 129-131) about the Hebrew idiom "I have come," an idiom denoting intent or purpose. One thing, however, must be emphasized again. When Jesus says "I have come," he is not referring to his Incarnation.

Undoubtedly, in trying to understand this passage, everything hinges on the meaning of the words "destroy" and "fulfill" in verse 17. What does Jesus mean by "destroy the Law" and "fulfill the Law"?

"Destroy" and "fulfill" are technical terms used in rabbinic argumentation. When a rabbi felt that his colleague had misinterpreted a passage of Scripture, he would say, "You are destroying the Law!" Needless to say, in most cases his colleague strongly disagreed. What was "destroying the Law" for one rabbi, was "fulfilling the Law" (correctly interpreting Scripture) for another.

What we see in Matthew 5:17 ff. is a rabbinic discussion. Someone has accused Jesus of "destroying" the Law. Of course, neither Jesus nor his accuser would ever think of literally destroying the Law. Furthermore, it would never enter the accuser's mind to charge Jesus with intent to abolish part or all of the Mosaic Law. What *is* being called into question is Jesus' system of interpretation, the way he interprets Scripture.

When accused, Jesus strongly denies that his method of interpreting Scripture "destroys," or weakens, its meaning. He claims, on the contrary, to be more orthodox than his accuser. For Jesus, a "light" commandment ("Do not bear hatred in your heart") is as important as a "heavy" commandment ("Do not murder").* And a brother who breaks even a "light" commandment will be considered "light" (have an inferior position) in Jesus' Movement (Matthew 5:19).

"Never imagine for a moment," Jesus says, "that I intent to abrogate the Law by misinterpreting it. My intent is not to weaken or negate the Law, but by properly interpreting God's Written Word I aim to establish it, that is, make it even more lasting. I would never invalidate the Law by effectively removing something from it through misinterpretation. Heaven and earth would sooner disappear than something from the Law. Not the smallest letter in the alphabet, the *yod,* nor even its decorative spur,** will ever disappear from the Law."

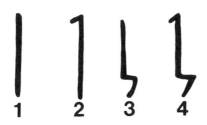

Fig. 31. The "tittle" of the jot *(yod)* is the small decorative spur projecting from the jot's upper edge. Other letters, for instance, the *lamed* (see illustration), can also have a "tittle." 1: jot   2: jot with tittle   3: lamed   4: lamed with tittle.

*Matthew 5:21-26 is the first of five examples given by Jesus to illustrate his method of interpreting Scripture. The commandment, "You shall not hate your brother in your heart," is found in Leviticus 19:17. The commandment, "You shall not murder," is found in Exodus 20:13 and Deuteronomy 5:17.

**The title of the *yod* is the small point projecting from its upper edge.

———————— • ————————

8. LUKE 6:22 (page 82) ''cast out your name as evil''

Here is another of the many Hebrew idioms which have been preserved in our English Gospels.* This idiom has not been preserved perfectly, since the word ''as'' is not part of the idiom. In Hebrew it is not ''name *as* evil'' (or ''bad''), but simply ''name bad'' *(shem rah)*. Why? Because in Hebrew adjectives follow nouns. In English one says ''narrow street.'' In Hebrew one says ''street narrow.'' In English one says ''bad name'' — in Hebrew, ''name bad.'' The Greek translator of the Hebrew Gospel was a firm believer in literal translations, but to write in Greek ''cast out your name bad'' was carrying things a little too far even for him. By translating ''cast out your name *as* bad,'' he hoped to make his translation more intelligible to his Greek readers.

There is a further difficulty. Even if we remove the word ''as,'' and correctly translate ''bad name'' instead of ''name bad,'' this expression is still not clear in English. What does ''cast out your bad name'' mean? ''Cast out'' is a very poor English translation, not because it is not a legitimate translation of the Greek verb used here, but because it is not a translation, as it should be, of the Hebrew equivalent of that Greek verb. As was customary, the Greek translator employed the fixed or standard Greek translation of a Hebrew word rather than trying to

*This idiom appears in the Old Testament in Deuteronomy 22:13, 19 (compare Nehemiah 6:13).

translate to idiomatic Greek.* Unfortunately for English translators of the New Testament, by and large equipped only with a knowledge of Greek, the Greek verb used here *(ekballo),* and its Hebrew equivalent *(hotzi),* do not have the same shades of meaning. This Greek verb does basically mean "cast out" or "throw out," but the Hebrew verb it translates seldom, if ever, has that meaning. The Hebrew verb *(hotzi)* is a causative form of a root meaning "go out." This form of the Hebrew verb may therefore be translated literally as "cause to go (or come) out"; but may also often mean "cause to go out" in the sense of "make public" or "publish." It is obvious that the latter meaning is demanded in this context.

"Publish (or publicize) your name bad" is simply a Hebrew way of saying "defame you," "malign you," or "slander you." The phrase traditionally translated in English by six words, "cast out your name as evil," is a Hebrew idiom which, if English translators would only seek Hebrew equivalents to the Greek, could be translated in English by only two words: "malign you." And should an English translator wish to find equivalent English idioms that preserve some of the literalness of the Hebrew expression, such as the word "name," he has at his disposal, in colloquial English, expressions such as "give you a bad name," or "smear your name."

"When you are slandered on my account," Jesus says "rejoice, for great is your reward in heaven."

---

*For an explanation of the method of translation employed in ancient times by Greek translators, see page 143.

———————— • ————————

9. LUKE 9:29 (page 82) "the fashion of his countenance was altered"

A much better English translation would be, "his face changed its appearance." The Greek reads, "the appearance of his face (was) different" — not elegant English, but at least intelligible. This time most of the difficulty is caused by the archaic English of the King James Version. The Revised Standard Version does not help matters. As usual, it departs only slightly from the King James translation, changing only one word: instead of "fashion," the Revised Standard Version has "appearance."

Although the expression "the fashion of his countenance" (literally, "the appearance of his face") looks Hebrew — two nouns are hooked together in a characteristically Hebrew fashion — it is not found in the Old Testament. We can be sure, however, that this expression is good Hebrew because it is found in the Hebrew literature contemporary with Jesus, in what is known as Rabbinic Literature.*

This story in the life of Jesus (Luke 9:28-36) is known as the Transfiguration, though the word "transfiguration" does not actually appear in the text. "Transfiguration" refers to the supernatural change in the appearance of Jesus described in verse 29. What actually happened to Jesus' face? Apparently, like his clothes, his

---

*The expression "the appearance of the face" is found twice in Sifre 2:103, and twice in Tosefta Sanhedrin 8:6.

face began to shine. This would have reminded Peter, James, and John of the way Moses looked whenever he spoke with the LORD. Moses' face shone when he came down from Mount Sinai (Exodus 34:29). Likewise, it shone each time he visited the Tabernacle (Exodus 34:34-35). The three disciples would also have remembered that whenever Moses entered the Tabernacle God spoke with him from a cloud (Exodus 33:9). Here, too, at the Transfiguration, God speaks from a cloud.

Moses and Elijah appeared and spoke with Jesus on the mountain. They represent the Law and the Prophets, the two most important divisions of the Hebrew Bible.* Moses represents the Law, the five books of Moses. Elijah represents the Prophets, in Jewish tradition the division of Scripture which includes the following 21 books: Joshua, Judges, I & II Samuel, I & II Kings, Isaiah, Jeremiah, Ezekiel, and "the Twelve" (the twelve minor prophets). Jesus is the fulfillment of the Law and the Prophets.

But Moses and Elijah are also the two great prophets of the Old Testament. Their appearance with Jesus emphasized his prophetic role. Moses had prophesied (Deuteronomy 18:15) that God would one day raise up another prophet like himself. That prophet was to be obeyed ("listened to").** All the Old Testament points to this great Prophet of the Last Days. Jesus was that prophet. Notice Heaven's response to Peter's suggestion that *three* booths be built: "This is My Son, My Chosen; *listen to him*" (Luke 9:35).

*The three divisions of the Hebrew Bible are: the Law, the Prophets, and the Writings.
**"Listen" in the sense of "obey" was briefly discussed on page 88.

———————— • ————————

10. LUKE 9:44 (page 82) "lay these sayings in your ears"

The above translation of these words of Jesus is· so "un-English" that it is almost a joke. The King James translators, as usual, have done nothing more than translate the Greek text word for word into English. It is unfair, though, to be too harsh in our criticism of them, since "dynamic" translation, that is, attempting to give the sense of the original rather than a word-for-word translation, is really only a phenomenon of the Twentieth century. When the Greek translator of the original *Life of Jesus* translated the above Hebrew expression word for word into Greek, he was employing the traditional method of translation. Almost 1600 years later, the translators commissioned by King James, still using the word-for-word method, translated that same expression from Greek into English; and thus it was that a beautiful Hebrew idiom was perpetuated in our English Gospels.

This idiom, "lay (or put) in the ears of," is found only one time in the Old Testament — in Exodus 17:14. After Israel's battle with Amalek* at Rephidim (Exodus 17:8-13), Moses was commanded by God to record in writing a very important promise: "I will thoroughly erase every trace of the people of Amalek." This prom-

---

*Amalek was a tribe in the southern part of the land, in the area bordering the Sinai desert. Because it opposed Israel's attempt to enter the "Promised Land," Amalek was especially odious to God, becoming the symbol of the archenemy of His people.

ise was so important that God wanted it documented, written down. He wanted to be absolutely sure it would be remembered. "Write this in a scroll as a *remembrance*" is what the text literally says. But not only did God command Moses to record the promise in writing, he also commanded Moses to *put* it *in the ears of* (i.e., "announce it to") Joshua. "Put in the ears of" implies more than just "reading" or "repeating" in the hearing of Joshua. Undoubtedly, this idiom also carries the added emphasis: "Listen carefully and remember well, for what you are about to hear is very important."

Why these extra precautions? Why did God take such pains to make sure this particular promise would be remembered? — because it is a warning as well as a promise. "I will thoroughly erase every trace of Amalek" implies that God will not immediately destroy the tribe of Amalek. As Moses explained, "The LORD will be at war with Amalek generation after generation" (Exodus 17:16).

And why was it that God commanded Moses to inform Joshua, and not someone else, of this promise/ warning? Because Joshua would be the one to fight the battles with Amalek. It was Joshua who needed to be warned about the difficulties he would face; and, of course, it was Joshua who also needed to be encouraged by the promise of ultimate victory over the enemy.

Moses made it clear (Exodus 17:16) that for generations to come there would be war between Israel and Amalek. History confirms the accuracy of that prophecy. From the wilderness times until the early monarchy Amalek was Israel's hereditary enemy. It was only after the victories of Saul and David that the

Amalekites finally ceased to be a threat to the southern borders of Judah.

Throughout his lifetime Joshua fought the Amalekites. Following that first battle at Rephidim God felt Joshua should know what lay ahead. There would be many more battles. Joshua would be severely tested, but he must not give up. One day the enemy, Amalek, would be forever defeated. In the meantime, Joshua would have to go on fighting. The war was not over — that was the warning. Israel would win the war — that was the promise.*

Is it by coincidence that in Luke 9:44 Jesus uses an expression ("lay in the ears of") which appears only one time in the Hebrew Bible? Spoken in a day when a majority of the Jews living in the Land of Israel knew the Hebrew Scriptures almost by heart, that seems unlikely. No, Jesus' use of this expression in addressing his disciples is not an accident. He places it just before these words:

> Behold, we are going up to Jerusalem, and everything that has been written by the Prophets about the Son of Man will be fulfilled: he will suffer, and be rejected by the elders, high priests and scribes, and be handed over to the Gentiles; he will be killed, but on the third day rise.**

These are momentous words. Little wonder that Jesus adds the preface: "Put these words in your ears!" In other words, "Listen very carefully to what I am about

* *Adonai-nissi* ("the LORD is my banner)" in Exodus 17:15 suggests a victory won with God's help.
**Reconstructed from three passages where Jesus tells the disciples about his coming death: Luke 9:22 (= Matthew 16:21); Luke 9:44 (= Matthew 17:22-23); Luke 18:31-32 (= Matthew 20:18-19).

to tell you, and keep it in mind in the days ahead.'' Jesus prefaces his words with an expression found in the Old Testament because it brings to mind the promise/warning God gave to Joshua. Jesus wishes to prepare his disciples for the persecution they will face after he is repudiated by the Jewish leaders and then executed as a criminal. At the same time, Jesus wishes to encourage the disciples by assuring them of his victory. (''He will be killed, but on the third day rise''). Nothing could have been more appropriate than for Jesus to preface his words with, than ''put these words in your ears.''

Like Joshua, the disciple of Moses, Jesus' disciples faced a severe test. Very soon they would be tempted to give up, to desert. The enemy, Satan, would not be kind. In spite of that, the disciples were not to lose heart, for God would *"utterly* blot out the memory of Amalek.''*

———————————— • ————————————

11. LUKE 9:51 (page 82) ''he set his face to go . . .''

The Hebrew language is especially fond of idioms which incorporate the names of the parts of the body: head, hands, feet, eyes, etc.** ''Face'' is also incorporated in scores of Hebrew idioms. Hagar fled from ''the

---

* In the Old Testament, Amalek, Israel's archenemy, symbolizes Satan.
** Hebrew, of course, is not the only language to use the names of the parts of the body in its idioms. All languages do this to some extent, though

face of" Sarai (Genesis 16:6,8); Jacob from "the face of" Esau (Genesis 35:1, 7); and Moses from "the face of" Pharaoh (Exodus 2:15); Moses "hid his face" in fear (Exodus 3:6); God sometimes "hides His face" in anger (Deuteronomy 31:17,18; Jeremiah 33:5). God "sets His face against" idolaters (Leviticus 20:3,5,6). He can "make His face shine upon" (deal kindly with) someone (Numbers 6:25, Psalms 31:16), or "turn away His face" (II Chronicles 30:9). Joseph, in grief, "fell on the face of" his father (Genesis 50:1). But, before a king, one falls on his own face (II Samuel 9:6). King Joash "wept over the face of" the dying Elisha (II Kings 13:14). Jehu "lifted up his face" to the window out of which Jezebel was looking (II Kings 9:32).

In Hebrew, faces can even walk! Moses was willing for God to bring him and the People of Israel to the Promised Land on condition that God's face would "walk" with them (Exodus 33:15).* It is also interesting that the expression, "the Angel of His *Face,*" is often used in Scripture as a synonym for "the Angel of the LORD" (Isaiah 63:9, et al). Note that in this expression, "His Face" is replaced by "His Presence" in almost all English versions of the Bible. "Presence," however, is only the attempt of English translators to give sense to the Hebrew word "face." Actually, in Hebrew, "His Face" is just another way of saying "the LORD." "The Angel of His Face" is an exact equiva-

---

*Notice the very same idiom ("his face was walking") in Luke 9:53, immediately following "he set his face to go."

**each language has its own unique idioms. English, for instance, has "lend an ear," "sharpen the ears," "give someone the eye" and "keep an eye out." We smile when we stop to think about the literal meaning of these idioms.

lent of "the LORD's Angel," and nothing more.

What reader of the King James Version of the Bible does not remember the famous "shewbread" (archaic English for "showbread")? These were the twelve loaves of bread baked every Sabbath eve and placed on a table in the Tabernacle. There they remained until the following Sabbath when they were replaced by fresh loaves (Exodus 25:30, *et al*). Later, in the temple Solomon built, these loaves lay on a table of gold (I Kings 7:48). Modern English translations of the Bible, such as the Revised Standard Version, generally prefer "bread of the Presence" to "shewbread"; but both "shewbread" and "bread of the Presence" result from the difficulty in translating a Hebrew "face" idiom — in this case, "bread of the *face*." As we would expect, the table on which the "bread of the *face*" rests is called the "table of the *face*" (Numbers 4:7).

The idiom used in Luke 9:51 is also a Hebrew "face" idiom. To "set one's face" simply means "turn in the direction of." This idiom appears several times in the Old Testament (II Kings 12:17; Daniel 11:17; Genesis 31:21). Just like the verb "turn" in English, "set one's face" can be followed by "to" in the sense of "toward"; or by "to" plus an infinitive (i.e., "to go," "to come," "to attack," etc.) as in Luke 9:51.

Apparently, none of our English translators recognized this Hebrew idiom in Luke 9:51. Most translations, even some of the most recent, have retained the word "face," and thus unwittingly transmitted a Hebraism. A few translators attempted to give a more English flavor: "he resolutely set out" (New International Version); "he resolutely took the road"

(Jerusalem Bible); ''he proceeded with fixed purpose'' (Weymouth); ''he moved steadily onward with an iron will'' (Living Bible). This unnecessary emphasis on resoluteness eventually resulted in the translation, ''As the days drew near when Jesus would be taken up to heaven, *he made up his mind* [italics the author's] and set out on his way to Jerusalem'' (Good News For Modern Man). From this last translation one might get the impression that Jesus, after much soul searching, at last decided to go through with his crucifixion — as if, until then, he had not been able to make up his mind.

The way translators have translated Luke 9:51 illustrates what happens when a translator of the Gospels is solely dependent on the Greek text and makes no effort to recover the Hebrew behind the Greek: his translation gets clogged with literalisms such as ''face.'' In the case of Luke 9:51, many translators were further misled by the verb of the idiom. Greek has several words for ''set.'' Because the ''set'' found in the Greek of Luke 9:51 carries ''fix'' or ''establish'' as its particular shade of meaning, translators began to insert the idea of *fixed* purpose. The Hebrew idiom, however, does not connote resoluteness or firmness of purpose.

How then should Luke 9:51 be translated? Literally, the text reads: ''And when the days of his ascension were fulfilled, and he put his face to go to Jerusalem.'' This is good Hebrew, but scarcely English. An accurate English translation would be: ''When the time came for him to be taken up to heaven, he headed for Jerusalem.'' In other words, when the time came, Jesus went. This verse is simple narration, a description of events. It should not be made to imply that Jesus, after an inner struggle, finally found the courage to go to Jerusalem.

———————————— • ————————————

12. LUKE 10:5-6 (page 83) "Whatever house you enter, first say, '*Shalom* be to this house.' And if a son
of *shalom* is there, your *shalom* shall rest upon him;
but if not, it shall return to you."
"Son of peace" is an idiom which does not exist in
English. To translate it literally, as do most of our Bible
translations, is of little help. What does "son of peace"
mean?

A few of the more recent translations of the Bible
have used "lover of peace" (Goodspeed, Good News
for Modern Man, Phillips). While that sounds more
English, it is not the correct translation of the Hebrew
idiom "son of peace."

The wide range of meaning of the Hebrew word
"son" has already been mentioned (see page 81). Actually, its range of meaning is even wider than was indicated: "son of a house" is one who is such a close friend
that he is like a member of the family; "son of death" (I
Samuel 20:31) is one who deserves to die, or who has
been condemned to die; "son of Gehinnom" is someone who is bound for Gehinnom (hell); "son of a conversation" is one's partner in a conversation; "son of
eating" is a thing which is fit to be eaten. And there are
many other idiomatic usages in Hebrew of the word
"son."

"Son of peace" does not refer to the peace-loving man (although he is probably that too), but rather to the friendly man, the man who gets along well with other people. This is the harmonious, good-natured person who simply loves other people. It is a person with an attitude like the well-known cowboy humorist, the late Will Rogers, who said, "I never met a man I didn't like." Naturally, a "son of peace" is cordial, warm-hearted, generous, and hospitable. Jesus instructs his disciples to bless the family of such a man. They are to remain in his home as long as they remain in his city. They are not to move from house to house. The implication is that if they *do not* find a "son of peace" in the house they have entered, they are to move to another house.

Let us try to express more fully what Jesus said in Luke 10:5-6 by translating freely into idiomatic English:

When you are invited into a home, let your first act be to say, "Peace to this family!"* If the head of the house turns out to be truly friendly and hospitable [a "son of peace"], let the blessing, "Peace," you pronounced when you entered his house remain upon his family. If he is not friendly, withdraw your blessing [and move to another house].

"Peace to this family" is the blessing. It is a blessing of *"shalom,"* or *"peace."* The Hebrew word *"shalom"* has shades of meaning the English word "peace" does not have. *"Shalom"* can mean "safety" or "security," as for instance in Luke 11:21, "When a

---

*Literally, "house," not "family," but in Hebrew "house" can also mean "household" or "family" (see the explanation on pages 80-81).

strong man, fully armed, guards his own house, his possessions are in *shalom* [i.e., "safe"]." A disciple of Jesus blessed his host with safety: while the disciple lodged in a home, the host and his family were safe, and all their possessions were safe. "*Shalom*" can also mean "good health." The disciple blessed his host with health; the disciple's presence meant protection against injury and illness. In addition, since each disciple healed the sick in whatever town or village he visited, certainly we may assume that he healed any sick members of a family with whom he had been invited to stay. His blessing, then, was not just empty words. He had a real and tangible blessing to give, so much so that Jesus said the disciple deserved payment for it (Luke 10:7). The blessing Jesus instructed his disciples to use reminds us of a similar blessing used by the rabbis: "*Shalom* to you, *shalom* to your house [i.e., "family"], and *shalom* to everything you own."

BIBLIOGRAPHY

Birkeland, Harris, "The Language of Jesus," *Avhandlinger utgitt av det Norske Videnskaps – Akademi i Oslo,* Vol. II, No. 1, 1954.

Black, Matthew. *An Aramaic Approach to the Gospels and Acts,* 3rd ed. Oxford, 1967.

Chill, Abraham. *The Mitzvot: The Commandments and Their Rationale.* Jerusalem, 1974.

Grintz, Jehoshua M. "Hebrew as the Spoken and Written Language in the Last Days of the Second Temple," *Journal of Biblical Literature,* Vol. LXXIX, 1960, 32-47.

Gromacki, Robert G. *New Testament Survey.* Grand Rapids, 1974.

Hatch, Edwin and Redpath, Henry A. *A Concordance to the Septuagint,* 2 vols. Oxford, 1897.

Lapide, Pinhas. "The Missing Hebrew Gospel," *Christian News From Israel,* Vol. XXIV, 1974, 167-170.

Lindsey, Robert L. *A Hebrew Translation of the Gospel of Mark,* 2nd ed. Jerusalem, 1973.

Meshorer, Ya'akov. *Jewish Coins of the Second Temple Period.* Tel Aviv, 1967.

Milik, M. L'Abbe' J. T. *Ten Years of Discovery in the Wilderness of Judea,* Translated from French by J. Strugnell. London, 1963.

Pines, Shlomo. *The Jewish Christians of the Early Centuries of Christianity According to a New Source.* Jerusalem, 1966.

Segal, M. H. *A Grammar of Mishnaic Hebrew.* Oxford, 1927.

Turner, Nigel. *Grammatical Insights into the New Testament.* Edinburgh, 1965.

Wrede, William. *Das Messiasgeheimnis in den Evangelien,* 2nd ed. Göttingen, 1913.

Yadin, Yigael. *Megillat ha-Miqdash (The Temple Scroll),* 3 vols. Jerusalem, 1977.

Ziegler, I. *Die Königsgleichnisse des Midrasch be leuchtet durch die römische Kaiserzeit.* Breslau, 1903.

NOTES

NOTES

NOTES

NOTES